Collins

EXPLORE ENGLISH

Student's Coursebook 5

William Collins' dream of knowledge for all began with the publication of his first book in 1819.
A self-educated mill worker, he not only enriched millions of lives, but also founded a flourishing publishing house. Today, staying true to this spirit, Collins books are packed with inspiration, innovation and practical expertise. They place you at the centre of a world of possibility and give you exactly what you need to explore it.

Collins. Freedom to teach.

An imprint of HarperCollins*Publishers*
The News Building
1 London Bridge Street
London SE1 9GF

HarperCollins*Publishers*
Macken House, 39/40 Mayor Street Upper,
Dublin 1, D01 C9W8, Ireland

Browse the complete Collins catalogue at
www.collins.co.uk

ISBN 978-0-00-836920-0

Authors: Robert Kellas, Sandy Gibbs, Kathryn Gibbs
Publisher: Elaine Higgleton
Product manager: Lucy Cooper
Series editor: Daphne Paizee
Development editor: Cait Hawkins
Project manager: Lucy Hobbs
Proof reader: Jo Kemp
Cover design by Gordon MacGilp
Cover artist: HarperCollins *Publishers* Ltd
© 2007 (Kes Gray)
Typesetting by QBS Learning
Illustrations by QBS Learning
Production controller: Lyndsey Rogers

Printed in India by Multivista Global Pvt. Ltd.

MIX
Paper | Supporting responsible forestry
FSC™ C007454
www.fsc.org

This book contains FSC™ certified paper and other controlled sources to ensure responsible forest management.

For more information visit: www.harpercollins.co.uk/green

Acknowledgements
The publishers gratefully acknowledge the permissions granted to reproduce copyright material in the book. Every effort has been made to contact the holders of copyright material, but if any have been inadvertently overlooked, the Publisher will be pleased to make the necessary arrangements at the first opportunity.

HarperCollins*Publishers* Limited for extracts and artwork from: *If It Wasn't For Tom* by Catherine MacPhail, illustrated by Francesco Ghersina, text © 2013 Catherine MacPhail. *In the Game* by Katy Coope, illustrated by Katy Coope, text © 2012 Katy Coope. *Harry the Clever Spider at School* by Julia Jarman, illustrated by Charlie Fowkes, text © 2007 Julia Jarman. *Mojo and Weeza and the Funny Thing* by Sean Taylor, illustrated by Julian Mosedale, text © 2005 Sean Taylor. *Mojo and Weeza and the New Hat* by Sean Taylor, illustrated by Julian Mosedale, text © 2007 Sean Taylor. *Where on Earth?* by Scoular Anderson, illustrated by Scoular Anderson, text © 2005 Scoular Anderson. *Horses' Holiday* by Kaye Umansky, illustrated by Ainslie Macleod, text © 2005 Kaye Umansky. *Olympic Heroes* by Jillian Powell, text © 2012 Jillian Powell. *First Day* by Kes Gray, illustrated by Korky Paul, text © 2007 Kes Gray.

Photo acknowledgements
The publishers wish to thank the following for permission to reproduce photographs. Every effort has been made to trace copyright holders and to obtain their permission for the use of copyright materials. The publishers will gladly receive any information enabling them to rectify any error or omission at the first opportunity.

(t = top, c = centre, b = bottom, r = right, l = left)

p15 Adrian Sherratt/Alamy, p21a Eric Isselee/Shutterstock, p21b Alexander Cher/Shutterstock, p21c LazyFocus/Shutterstock, p21d Stephen Mcsweeny/Shutterstock, p21e Catmando/Shutterstock, p21f nattanan726/Shutterstock, p21g Christian Musat/Shutterstock, p21h Neirfy/Shutterstock, p21i apple2499/Shutterstock, p21j Aaron Amat/Shutterstock, p21k Eric Isselee/Shutterstock, p21l Eric Isselee/Shutterstock, p23l Jiang Zhongyan/Shutterstock, p23cl 7th Son Studio/Shutterstock, p23cr Rich Carey/Shutterstock, p23r Catmando/Shutterstock, p38a Michal Sanca/Shutterstock, p38b Kluva/Shutterstock, p38c grynold/Shutterstock, p38d Snap2Art/Shutterstock, p38e teolin/Shutterstock, p38f Marko Rupena/Shutterstock, p38g Snap2Art/Shutterstock, p38h Michal Sanca/Shutterstock, p38i Michal Sanca/Shutterstock, p38j weter 777/Shutterstock, p38k opel/Shutterstock, p38l Icons shop/Shutterstock, p44 Diego Schutman/Shutterstock, p65 13FTStudio/Shutterstock, p68l leungchopan/Shutterstock, p68cl Fabiana Ponzi/Shutterstock, p68cr SpeedKingz/Shutterstock, p68r MIA Studio/Shutterstock, p76 Jonas Gratzer/LightRocket/Getty, p102 Yuri Yavnik/Shutterstock, p103tl Eric Isselee/Shutterstock, p103tc MO_SES Premium/Shutterstock, p103c Stockforliving/Shutterstock, p103cr Timolina/Shutterstock, p109a MO_SES Premium/Shutterstock, p109b Whitevector/Shutterstock, p109c topseller/Shutterstock, p109d Nerthuz/Shutterstock, p109e Tommy Alven/Shutterstock, p109f Vladyslav Starozhylov/Shutterstock, p109g Rawpixel.com/Shutterstock, p109h Chesky/Shutterstock, p109i Iakov Filimonov/Shutterstock, p109j 3DMAVR/Shutterstock, p109k Vereshchagin Dmitry/Shutterstock, p132a cigdem/Shutterstock, p132b Petr Kratochvil/Shutterstock, p132c Lightspring/Shutterstock, p132d DesignPie.cc/Shutterstock, p132e suns07butterfly/Shutterstock, p132f Kobkob/Shutterstock, p132g Suzanne Tucker/Shutterstock, p132h Vertes Edmond Mihai/Shutterstock, p132i Webspark/Shutterstock, p132j topseller/Shutterstock, p132k Chiyacat/Shutterstock, p147t GEORGES GOBET/AFP/Getty, p147b Ker Robertson/Getty Images Sport/Getty, p148 TOSHIO SAKAI/AFP/Getty

With thanks to the following teachers and schools for reviewing materials in development:
Hawar International School; Melissa Brobst, International School of Budapest; Niki Tzorzis, Pascal Primary School Lemessos.

Contents

Unit 1 Talking about people

Week 1 About me

1 Complete this information sheet about yourself.

My name is _____.

I come from _____ and live in _____.

My family:

_____

_____

My hobbies:

_____

_____

_____

My favourite ...

colour is _____.

subject is _____.

sport is _____.

food is _____.

2 **Read about Maria on page 4 in the Student's Resource Book. Match the questions to the correct answers.**

a) What is your name?   I am from the Philippines.

b) Where are you from?   Yes, I have two older brothers.

c) Do you have any brothers or sisters?   I live with my mum and brothers.

d) What is your favourite subject?   My name is Maria.

e) What is your hobby?   I love surfing!

f) Who do you live with?   My favourite subject is science.

3 **Read about Bolin on page 4 in the Student's Resource Book. Fill in the missing words.**

Bolin was born in _____, but now he lives with a _____ in London. He attends _____ school in London to practise _____. He has three hobbies: reading _____, building _____ and playing _____.

4 **Read about Amira and Ashira on page 5 in the Student's Resource Book. Answer these questions in full sentences.**

a) Where are Amira and Ashira from?

_____

b) What does Amira's name mean in English?

_____

c) Where do they play after school?

_____

d) What does Amira love eating?

_____

5 **Read about João on page 5 in the Student's Resource Book. Write three sentences about him.**

_____

_____

_____

_____

6 **Read about Siyabonga on page 5 in the Student's Resource Book. Write three sentences about him.**

_____

_____

_____

_____

7 **Who would say this? Circle the correct answer.**

1   "I love flying my kite!"   **a)** Ashira   **b)** João   **c)** Siyabonga

2   "I love wearing pink clothes!"   **a)** João   **b)** Siyabonga   **c)** Amira

3   "I love reading and drawing!"   **a)** Siyabonga   **b)** João   **c)** Amira

4   "I don't like swimming."   **a)** Ashira   **b)** Siyabonga   **c)** João

8 **Create an imaginary character. Fill in this fact file.**

My name is _____ .

I am from _____ .

I live with _____ .

I am in _____ .

My favourite colours are _____ .

I like _____ , but I don't like _____ .

9 **Write a short description of your character.**

_____

_____

_____

_____

_____

_____

_____

_____

10 Read pages 4 and 5 in the Student's Resource Book. Find other words you can use to talk about what you like and don't like doing.

Like _____   Don't like _____

_____   _____

_____   _____

11 Use the words you wrote in Activity 10, to describe some of the things you like or don't like doing at home.

1: _____

2: _____

3: _____

4: _____

5: _____

6: _____

12 Ask three of your classmates what they like or dislike doing after school or on the weekend. Write their answers below.

Classmate A (Likes) _____

_____

(Dislikes) _____

_____

Classmate B (Likes) _____

_____

(Dislikes) _____

_____

Classmate C (Likes) _____

_____

(Dislikes) _____

_____

Week 2 Setting and achieving goals

1   **Listen to _Katie's Krops_. Circle the correct answer.**

   1   What did Katie do in the third grade?

   a) Ate a cabbage   **b)** Planted a cabbage   **c)** Doesn't say

   2   What did Katie do with the cabbage?

   a) Donated it to a soup kitchen   **b)** Decorated it with soup **c)** Doesn't say

   3   How old was Katie when she grew her first cabbage.

   a) 12 years old   **b)** 9 years old   **c)** Doesn't say

   4   What does Katie want to be when she grows up.

   a) A doctor   **b)** A chef   **c)** Doesn't say

2   **Answer these questions. Try to answer in full sentences.**

   a)   Which grade was Katie in when she planted her first cabbage seedling?

   _____

   b)   How big did the cabbage grow?

   _____

   c)   Why did Katie plant a vegetable patch?

   _____

   d)   How many gardens does Katie have now?

   _____

   e)   What is Katie's first book called?

   _____

3   **Change the verbs below into the past form.**

   Example: listen → listened

   a)   plant → _____   **b)**   grow → _____

   c)   make → _____   **d)**   know → _____

   e)   use → _____   **f)**   donate → _____

   g)   volunteer → _____   **h)**   feed → _____

   i)   help → _____   **j)**   decide → _____

4 **Read _Kid President_ on page 7 in the Student's Resource Book. Circle the correct answer for each statement.**

1   Kid President wants everyone to be happy.

    a) Right   **b)** Wrong   **c)** Doesn't say

2   Kid President made his first video in his bedroom.

    a) Right   **b)** Wrong   **c)** Doesn't say

3   Kid President has a YouTube channel and a website.

    a) Right   **b)** Wrong   **c)** Doesn't say

4   Kid President's real name is Brad Montague.

    a) Right   **b)** Wrong   **c)** Doesn't say

5   Kid President's sister loves watching his videos.

    a) Right   **b)** Wrong   **c)** Doesn't say

5 **Circle the correct answer.**

1   When was Robby born?

    a) In 2012   **b)** In 2004   **c)** In 2007

2   Robby has a problem called osteogenesis imperfecta. This means that:

    a) He never breaks his bones.

    b) He has very strong bones.

    c) His bones break very easily.

3   Robby and Brad are an internet sensation. This means that:

    a) They are very popular on the internet.

    b) They sing songs together online.

    c) They are not famous.

6 **Answer these questions.**

a) What is Kid President's real name? _____

b) Who made the first video with Robby? _____

c) What is Robby's book called? _____

d) What does Robby teach people? _____

e) What does Robby believe? _____

7 **Read the information and look at the table. Match the chores to the pictures. Tick the chores you do at home.**

Information: A chore is a small task that we do regularly. It can be at home, school or anywhere. Chores help our families and teachers. *Every morning, I tidy my room. Every evening, I wash the dishes.*

A sweep	**B** mop	**C** make	**D** feed	**E** cook	**F** vacuum
G wipe	**H** wash	**I** pick up	**J** fold	**K** hang up	**L** throw away

E dinner _____ the floor _____ the bed _____ the carpet

☐ ☐ ☐ ☐

_____ clothes _____ the cat _____ the laundry _____ dirty clothes

☐ ☐ ☐ ☐

_____ the table _____ the garbage _____ the washing _____ the floor

☐ ☐ ☐ ☐

8 **Listen to Siyabonga talk about his day. Write three things that are on his to-do list.**

To do:

_____

_____

_____

9 **Read *Katie's Krops* again. Look at her to-do list below. Add two more things to her list.**

> *To-do* lists are a great way to set small goals and to remember the things you have to do.

To do:

Buy seeds

Water vegetables

Check if cabbages are ready to pick

Cook soup

_____

_____

10 **Make two to-do lists. List four chores you will do at home and at school this week.**

At home:

_____

_____

_____

At school:

_____

_____

_____

11 **What are your goals? Complete this table.**

Goals for today:

Today, I want to _____

Today, I want to _____.

Goals for this year:

This year, I want to _____.

This year, I want to _____.

Goals for my future:

In the future, I want to _____.

In the future, I want to _____.

12 **Some goals are easy to achieve, but others are more difficult.**

Write your goals on the ladder from the easiest to achieve (bottom step) to the most difficult to achieve (top step).

13 **Complete the steps that help you plan for success.**

STEP 1: Understand yourself.

Make a list of things you can do well.

Make a list of things you can't do well.

I can do these things well.

_____

_____

_____

I can't do these things well yet.

_____

_____

_____

STEP 2: Choose a goal.

My goal is _____.

STEP 3: Make a plan.

Draw a picture of yourself now.

Draw a picture of yourself in the future.

What can you do to make your goal come true?

Now:		In the future:
I can...		I will...
I can...		I will...

STEP 4: Set a time limit.

By which date do you want to achieve your goal?

I will reach my goal by _____.

14 **Read this information about James Dyson.**

Dream Big!

The Dyson vacuum cleaner was designed and created by James Dyson. He came up with the idea to create it many years ago, but it took a long time for his idea to become a reality. He didn't like the regular vacuum cleaners that you can buy at most stores. Those vacuum cleaners would lose sucking power when they collected dust. The more dust the vacuum cleaner collected in its bag, the weaker it would become. He thought to himself, "There must be a better way to do this!"

His big idea was to create a vacuum cleaner that didn't need a bag — it could collect dust but wouldn't lose power. He tried 5,126 times to make the perfect vacuum cleaner, but failed every time! Finally, his 5,127th vacuum cleaner was perfect. He had created a very different type of vacuum cleaner. It didn't need a bag. His next challenge was to try and sell his idea. He took his new vacuum cleaner to different stores, but no one in the UK wanted to buy it. His machine was too different. No one wanted to take a risk with something so different.

James didn't give up. He believed his vacuum cleaner was a great idea. He took it to Japan, where they love technology. He won an award for his idea. But still, no one wanted to make and sell his vacuum cleaner. So what did he do? He started his own company! It took him 15 years to finally get his vacuum cleaner into shops, and today he is worth more than $3 billion. James Dyson had a dream and he worked very hard to achieve his dream. He failed many times, but finally he was successful.

15 **Circle the correct answer.**

1 James Dyson created a

   a) television.

   b) vacuum cleaner.

2 His creation was different because

   a) it didn't need a bag.

   b) it could suck up dirt.

3 It took James Dyson 15 years

   a) to become the richest man in the world.

   b) to get his vacuum cleaner into stores.

4 Today, James Dyson

   a) has his own successful company.

   b) is worth less than three billion dollars.

16 Answer these questions.

a) What did James Dyson design and create?

_____

b) Why did he want to create this?

_____

c) How many times did James Dyson fail? _____

d) In which countries did James Dyson try to sell his machine? _____

e) Why did he choose Japan? _____

17 Fill in the missing words.

James _____ designed and created a _____ _____. It is called

_____ _____ _____ _____. His vacuum

cleaner doesn't need a _____. He failed _____ times before he was successful.

Finally, his vacuum cleaner was perfect! But no one would sell it because it was

too _____. He went to _____ because this country loves

_____. He won an _____. But still, no one would sell it.

Then he started his own _____. Now he is very rich and his vacuum

cleaner is very famous!

Week 3 Tell me more

1 **Complete the questions. Choose words from the box to help you.**

> How long   How often   What   When   Where   Which   Why   Who

a) _____ am I meant to brush my teeth in 24 hours?

b) _____ have you lived in this house?

c) _____ is your favourite colour?

d) _____ do you live?

e) _____ is the shortest person in your family?

f) _____ do you like more, bananas or strawberries?

g) _____ is your birthday?

h) _____ are the names of your friends?

i) _____ can I do to help you today?

j) _____ is a good time to brush your teeth?

k) _____ helps you when you are sick?

l) _____ do children go to school?

2 **Answer the questions above.**

a) _____

b) _____

c) _____

d) _____

e) _____

f) _____

g) _____

h) _____

i) _____

j) _____

k) _____

l) _____

3 **Circle your answer.**

    a) Do you like pizza?   Yes, I do.   No, I don't.

    b) Do you have a sister?   Yes, I do.   No, I don't.

    c) Can you play a musical instrument?   Yes, I can.   No, I can't.

    d) Are you hungry?   Yes, I am.   No, I'm not.

    e) Is your birthday this week?   Yes, it is.   No, it isn't.

4 **Ask your partner these questions. Write their answers.**

    a) Do you like sport? _____

    b) Can you play soccer? _____

    c) Are you happy today? _____

    d) Do you have a pet? _____

    e) Can you make a sandwich? _____

    f) Are you a teacher? _____

5 **Read this information about questions. Give more examples of both types of questions.**

> There are two types of questions.
>
> **Closed questions** can be answered in one word (or a short phrase). The most common closed questions can be answered with "yes" or "no", like the questions you answered on this page. They are helpful if you want to know a simple fact. For example:
>
> Do you like tea?   No.
>
> Are you in Grade 5?   Yes.
>
> What is your name?   Fred.
>
> **Open questions** give your partner a chance to give a longer answer. These questions are helpful if you want more information about someone. The most common open questions are "Why?" and "How?" For example:
>
> Why do you like sport?   I like it because …
>
> How did you do that?   I did that by …

6 **Are these questions open or closed? Circle the correct answer.**

a) Are you feeling better today? open / closed

b) Can I go to the bathroom? open / closed

c) What do you plan to do when you get home today? open / closed

d) What is your favourite movie? open / closed

e) Have you finished your homework? open / closed

f) How did you and your best friend meet? open / closed

g) Would you like to go to the movies tonight? open / closed

h) How can I improve my maths skills? open / closed

i) Does four plus four equal eight? open / closed

j) Why do I have to finish my homework? open / closed

7 **Read this interview. Look at the questions the interviewer asks Kathy.**

Interviewer: Do you have any hobbies?

Kathy: Yes. I like to sing and dance.

Interviewer: Nice! How long have you been singing and dancing for?

> Closed questions are a good way to start an interview. They help you get some basic information. Then you can ask open questions to get more information.

Kathy: For two years.

Interviewer: Why did you choose singing and dancing as hobbies?

Kathy: One reason is because I like music. I also love to watch music videos, and my favourite artists always dance very well. I wish I could dance like them.

Interviewer: Who is your favourite music artist?

Kathy: Katy Perry.

Interviewer: Yes, she is very popular! Why do you like her so much?

Kathy: Oh, for four reasons. Firstly, she has a beautiful voice. Secondly, she wears cool clothes. Thirdly, she works very hard and lastly, she often helps poor people.

Interviewer: What would you do if you met Katy Perry?

Kathy: Oh, wow! I'm not sure. First, I would probably scream because I would be so excited. Then I think I would ask her to take a photograph with me so I could show my friends that I REALLY met her!

8 **Write down three closed questions from this interview.**

_____

_____

_____

9 **Write down three open questions from this interview.**

_____

_____

_____

10 **Ask your partner the questions you wrote.**

11 **Read the interview with Bolin on page 9 in the Student's Resource Book.**

a) Write three more closed questions you could ask Bolin.

_____

_____

_____

b) Write what you think he would answer.

_____

_____

_____

c) Write three more open questions you could ask him.

_____

_____

_____

12   **Create your own interview. Add three more questions to the interview below.**

Notice how each closed question is followed by an open question. Follow the same pattern with your questions.

My name: _____

Today, I am interviewing: _____

What is your favourite outdoor activity? _____ (closed)

Why? _____ (open)

What game do you like to play? _____ (closed)

How do you play it? _____ (open)

What do you want to do when you grow up? _____ (closed)

Why? _____ (open)

What is your goal for this year? _____ (closed)

How will you achieve it? _____ (open)

_____
_____ (closed)

_____
_____ (open)

_____
_____ (closed)

13   **Interview your partner.**

Unit 2 Amazing animals

Week 1 **Predators**

1   **Listen to the animal names. Find and label each animal.**

bear	cheetah	cobra	crocodile	dolphin	hawk	hyena
	lion	orca whale	shark	tiger	wolf	

_____ ☐   _____ ☐   _____ ☐   _____ ☐

_____ ☐   _____ ☐   _____ ☐   _____ ☐

_____ ☐   _____ ☐   _____ ☐   _____ ☐

2   **Tick the animals you hear about in _Predators!_**

3   **Complete this table.**

Predator	Prey
Orca	
African lion	

4   Read this information about predators. Write the correct answer.

Predators eat _____ (flowers / meat) to survive. They must be very fast to _____ (catch / play with) their prey. Usually they have very good eyes and _____ (clean / sharp) teeth. Some predators hunt in groups and work together as a _____ (team / friend). A good example of a predator is a _____ (cheetah / rabbit).

5   Underline the best definition.

hunt	**a)** to chase and kill wild animals for food	**b)** to see other animals in the dark
intelligent	**a)** to have very good eyes	**b)** to be clever or smart
environment	**a)** the natural place where an animal lives	**b)** food that predators eat
escape	**a)** to get away from danger	**b)** the place where wolves sleep

6   Answer the following questions.

a) Why do predators eat other animals?

_____

b) Give two examples of predators that live in water.

_____

c) Why do orcas hunt in groups?

_____

d) Why can lions hunt in the dark?

_____

e) What do lions usually do during the day?

_____

7   Read this information.

The **topic** tells you what the text is about in one or two words. It is 'what' or 'who' the text is *all* about. Usually the word is repeated many times.

The **main idea** tells you the important point about the topic. Ask yourself, "What does all this information tell me about the topic?" Often, the first or last sentence will tell you what the main idea is.

Details give you extra information about the topic.

Snow leopard

A snow leopard is able to live in very cold places. It has a thick coat to keep it warm. When it is very cold, the snow leopard wraps its long tail around itself like a scarf. Fur protects the snow leopard's wide feet from the freezing cold.

Polar bear

Polar bears are different from other bears. First, they don't sleep all winter. Second, they only eat meat and like to hunt seals. Third, polar bears don't have eyelashes. Fourth, they have webbed paws (skin between their toes) to help them swim better. And finally, if you shaved a polar bear you would see its skin is actually black.

The food chain

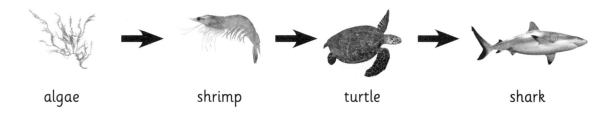

algae   shrimp   turtle   shark

All living things are part of the food chain. Every plant, insect, bird and animal needs energy to live and grow. Plants get energy from the Sun and from the ground. Some animals get energy when they eat plants. For example, a rabbit eats lettuce and carrots. Some animals must eat other animals, like the fox that eats the rabbit. And when the fox dies, its body breaks down and goes back into the earth.

8 Fill in the missing topics. Underline the correct main idea for each.

Text	Snow leopard	Polar bear	The food chain
Topic	snow leopards	_____	_____
Main idea	It is difficult to live in cold places. A long tail keeps snow leopards warm. Snow leopards are good at living in cold places. Snow leopards have big feet.	Polar bears like to sleep all winter. Polar bears are not like other bears. Polar bears are similar to other bears. Polar bears like to shave.	The fox must eat the rabbit. The fox is part of the food chain. All living things are in the food chain. Birds are not in the food chain.

9 Complete this table. Write four more details about polar bears.

Polar bears don't sleep all winter.				

10 Read the information about the orca on page 11 in the Student's Resource Book. Complete this diagram.

Topic:

Main idea:

Detail:	Detail:	Detail:	Detail:

11 **Underline the verbs in this paragraph. Circle the adverbs.**

I have an old grandfather. He walks so slowly and carefully.
Sometimes he needs ten minutes to cross a busy street. He is
the kindest man I know. He talks kindly to everyone he meets.
He loves to walk peacefully on sunny days in the park with my
little cousin, Jerry. Jerry runs around quickly. My slow grandfather can't catch him.
I like to walk quietly next to him so that I can listen to his interesting stories. I can
also help him catch Jerry when it is time to go home.

Adverbs describe verbs.

12 **Choose five adverbs that you circled and use them in sentences.**

a) _____

b) _____

c) _____

d) _____

e) _____

13 **Read the story about Leona on page 12 in the Student's Resource Book. Complete this table with adverbs and the verbs they describe. Draw a picture to illustrate one of the adverbs.**

Verbs	Adverbs

Week 2 Crazy creatures

1   **Read *No water? No problem!* on page 14 in the Student's Resource Book. There are spelling mistakes in these sentences. Write them correctly.**

    a)   Gerenuks live in desserts in Eest Africa.

    _____

    b)   A gerenuk standes on too legs to eet.

    _____

    c)   A gerenuk has a ferry longe nek.

    _____

    d)   They do'nt need watter to drink.

    _____

2   **Listen to the information about gerenuks. Fill in the missing words.**

> Africa   alone   antelope   beautiful   day   dry   fruit   interesting
> lonely   neck   peaceful   shade   small   water

    a)   Have you heard of a gerenuk? This long-necked _____ lives in the

    desert in East _____. It likes to stand on two legs to eat. Gerenuks

    can live in very _____ places because they never have to drink

    _____!

    b)   Gerenuks look for food during the _____. They usually sleep

    in the _____ in the afternoon. They eat leaves, flowers and

    _____. Gerenuks can reach very high in the trees because they have

    a long _____. I think they are very _____ animals.

c) Gerenuks are different from other antelopes. They like to live in very _____ groups. Usually, only three or four gerenuks will live together. Sometimes, a male gerenuk will choose to live _____. In my opinion, a life alone would be very _____. I like to live with other people.

d) These animals are very _____. They don't fight often. I think gerenuks are very _____.

3 **Read this information. Circle the adjectives.**

Look at the cute Gobi jerboa. These rodents live in the desert. Even though they are small, their bodies are perfect for their environment. They are well adapted. The Gobi jerboa has very large ears so it can

Adjectives describe nouns.

hear extremely well. It can smell really well too. Their eyes are big so they can see at night. Their tail is extremely long and is used for balancing. It can jump very far, sometimes up to three metres, because of its long back legs.

4 **Find synonyms in the paragraph above to match these words.**

Synonyms are words that mean the same.

ideal – _____

sweet – _____

little – _____

big – _____

rear – _____

very – _____

5 **Use each word from Activity 4 in a sentence.**

_____

_____

_____

_____

_____

_____

6   **Write 'fact' or 'opinion' next to these statements about gerenuks.**

a)   Gerenuks are interesting animals. _____

b)   The gerenuk is a long-necked antelope. _____

c)   They are very beautiful animals. _____

d)   They stand on two legs to eat. _____

e)   Sometimes, a male gerenuk chooses to live alone. _____

f)   A life alone is very lonely. _____

A fact is something that can be tested and is always true.

An opinion is a personal view. It is not always true.

7   **Choose the correct adjective for each sentence.**

a)   boring / bored:

Joe finds TV shows about animals _____.

Joe is _____ by TV shows about animals.

b)   amazing / amazed:

Mia is _____ at the leaf-tailed gecko's camouflage.

Mia thinks the leaf-tailed gecko's camouflage is _____.

c)   interested / interesting

Mikael thinks gerenuks are _____ animals.

Mikael is _____ in animals that live in deserts.

d) amused / amusing

Jenna was _____ by the Gobi jerboa's big ears.

Jenna found the Gobi jerboa's big ears _____.

e) frightened / frightening

I don't like big spiders. They are _____.

I am _____ of big spiders.

8   Listen to *The tiny tarsier*. Write two new facts about the tarsier.

_____

_____

9   Complete these sentences about the speaker's opinion.

a)   The speaker thinks that the tarsier is the _____ animal in the world.

b)   The speaker believes that humans must _____.

10   Are these sentences true or false? If the sentence is false, rewrite it. Change the underlined word to make it true.

Example: The tarsier is one of the biggest primates in the world.

False: The tarsier is one of the smallest primates in the world.

a)   This animal has really big eyes. Its eyes are smaller than its brain.

_____ : _____

b)   Their big ears help them to see in the dark.

_____ : _____

c)   Tarsiers love to eat birds.

_____ : _____

d)   The speaker believes that people must stop cutting down forests.

_____ : _____

11   **Work with a partner.**

a)   **Student A:** Read aloud *The tiny tarsier* from page 14 in the Student's Resource Book. Together, find three facts about the tarsier.

_____

_____

_____

What is your opinion of the tarsier?

I think the tarsier is _____ because

_____.

My partner thinks the tarsier is _____ because

_____.

b) **Student B:** Read aloud *The tardigrade* from page 15 in the Student's Book. Together, find three facts about the tardigrade.

_____

_____

_____

What is your opinion of the tardigrade?

I think the tardigrade is _____ because

_____.

My partner thinks the tardigrade is _____ because

_____.

12   **Compare the four weird and wonderful creatures on pages 14–15 in the Student's Resource Book. Circle the correct answer.**

a) The gerenuk is (bigger / biggest) than the tardigrade and the leaf-tailed gecko. It is also the animal with the (longer / longest) neck.

b) It might be small, but the tardigrade has (more / the most) legs than any of the other creatures. It can also survive in the (hotter / hottest) and (colder / coldest) temperatures.

c) The leaf-tailed gecko is (smaller / smallest) than the gerenuk. It is also (more / most) difficult to find, because it is very good at hiding between leaves.

d) Many people think the tarsier is the (cuter / cutest) creature because it is so small and has very big eyes. It is (smaller / smallest) than an adult human hand, but definitely (bigger / biggest) than a tardigrade.

13 Read all the articles about weird and wonderful animals again on pages 14–15 in the Student's Resource Book. Answer these questions with your opinion.

a) Which animal is the most interesting? _____

Why? _____

b) Which animal do you think is the cutest? _____

Why? _____

c) Which animal do you think is the smartest? _____

Why? _____

d) Which animal would you like as a pet? _____

Why? _____

14 Write about your favourite animal. Include facts and opinions.

_____

_____

_____

_____

_____

_____

_____

_____

15 Listen to the *The tardigrade*. Are these sentences fact or opinion?

a) A tardigrade is very strong. _____

b) It can live without food or water for 30 years. _____

c) The name 'water bear' is the best. _____

d) Tardigrades can live under the sea. _____

e) They are the most incredible animals on Earth. _____

f) A tardigrade has been to space. _____

Week 3 Animal stories

1   **Read the play about *Tiddalik the Thirsty Frog* on pages 16–17 in the Student's Resource Book. Answer the questions.**

a) Where is the play set?

_____

b) Why was Tiddalik grumpy?

_____

c) What did Tiddalik do?

_____

d) Colour the words that describe an action in the play.

awkwardly	drank	enthusiastically	greedily	grumpily

heavily	quickly	swelled	thirstily	tired

e) Circle the correct word in each sentence.

Tiddalik drank the water in the water hole (before / after) he drank the stream water.

Tiddalik drank the water in the lake (before / after) he drank the stream water.

Kangaroo nudged Tiddalik (before / after) Kookaburra told a funny joke.

The emus tried to make Tiddalik laugh (before / after) the lizards' clumsy dance.

f) How did Tiddalik's actions affect the environment?

_____

g) Did Tiddalik behave fairly? Give a reason for your answer.

_____

h) Did the animals treat Tiddalik kindly? Give a reason for your answer.

_____

2 **Discuss this question in small groups and then share your ideas with the class.**

What would your group do to try and make Tiddalik laugh?

Use this frame to help you.

First, …   Then, …   Next, …   After that, …   Finally, …

3 **Listen to the story *Tiddalik the Thirsty Frog*. Read the sentences and then circle the correct answer.**

1 Eel was unhappy because the sand was hot.

   a) Right   **b)** Wrong   **c)** Doesn't say

2 Kookaburra made Tiddalik laugh.

   a) Right   **b)** Wrong   **c)** Doesn't say

3 Tiddalik was happy that the water came pouring out of his mouth to fill the streams, lakes and watering holes.

   a) Right   **b)** Wrong   **c)** Doesn't say

4 Eel was happy to have water to swim in again.

   a) Right   **b)** Wrong   **c)** Doesn't say

4 **Here are the answers to some questions about the story *Tiddalik the Thirsty Frog*.**

Write the question that you think was asked.

_____

_____

_____

_____

Kangaroo's foot nudged Tiddalik.

Kookaburra's joke was funny.

Lizard's dance was clumsy.

Kangaroo's hops were high.

5   **Cross out the wrong word in each sentence.**

   a)   There are many (beautiful / beautifully) animals at the zoo.

   b)   Hurry up! You are walking very (slow / slowly).

   c)   The (loud / loudly) noise woke me up.

   d)   You can speak English very (good / well).

   e)   Be (careful / carefully) with that bag! There are eggs inside it.

   f)   It was a very (good / well) story.

6   **Complete these sentences. Use the correct form of the words in the box to help you.**

You have to change some of the words a little.

| close   fast   hard   neat   safe   terrible |

   a)   It is easy to read her story because she writes very _____.

   b)   Look _____ at these footprints. What animal made them?

   c)   My brother just started piano lessons. He plays _____.

   d)   He works _____, so he always passes all of his tests.

   e)   I was very scared to walk alone at night, but I got home _____.

   f)   I ran so _____ in the race, but I still didn't win.

7   **Complete these sentences with the correct words.**

   a)   _____ (Excitedly / The most excited), she opened her presents on her birthday.

   b)   Of all the animals, the cheetah can run _____ (the faster / the fastest).

   c)   At the end of term, the students walked home from school _____ (happily / more happily) than usual.

   d)   Jojo walked _____ (less quickly / the least quickly) than the others and had to run to catch the bus.

   e)   The lion ran _____ (more fast / faster) than the zebra and managed to catch it.

8 Fill in this diagram about *Tiddalik the Thirsty Frog*. Choose the details you think are important to include.

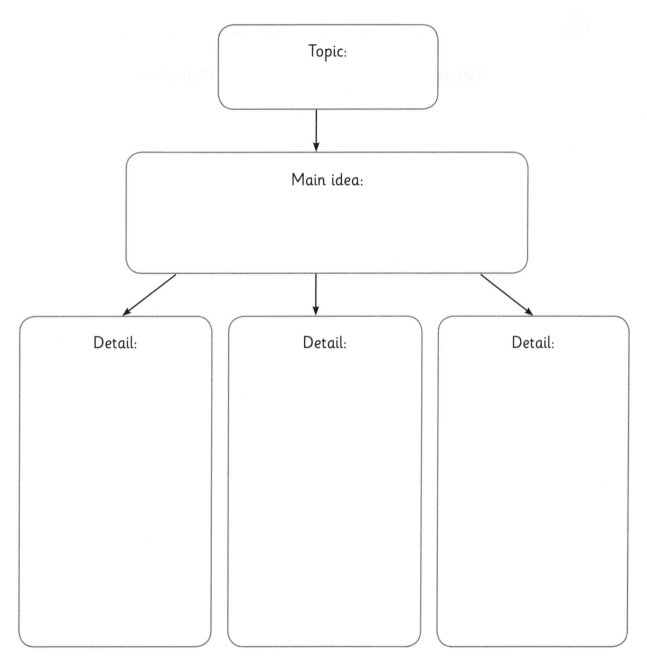

Topic:

Main idea:

Detail:

Detail:

Detail:

9 Work in pairs. Retell the story *Tiddalik the Thirsty Frog*. Try to use all these words in the story. Tick the words you hear your partner use.

☐ after   ☐ after that   ☐ and   ☐ because   ☐ so

☐ but   ☐ finally   ☐ next   ☐ then   ☐ when

10 Plan a story.

Title: _____

Setting	Characters

Beginning	Middle	End

11 **Write your story. Don't forget to check your spelling and punctuation when you've finished.**

_____

_____

_____

_____

_____

_____

_____

_____

_____

_____

_____

_____

_____

_____

_____

_____

_____

_____

_____

_____

_____

_____

_____

_____

Check your punctuation. Have you used:

— capital letters for names?

— speech marks for direct speech?

Unit 3 Sports and games

Week 1 International sports

1   **Match the sport to the picture. Write the name of the sport under each picture.**

| athletics | badminton | baseball | basketball | cricket | cycling |
| golf | hockey | rugby | soccer | swimming | tennis |

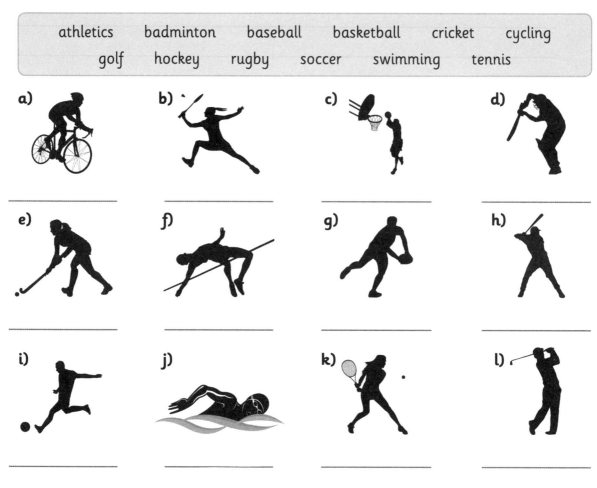

a) _____ b) _____ c) _____ d) _____

e) _____ f) _____ g) _____ h) _____

i) _____ j) _____ k) _____ l) _____

2   **Answer these questions using the sports names above.**

a) Can you name two sports where you kick the ball?

_____ and _____ .

b) Can you name three sports that use a stick or bat to hit the ball?

_____ , _____ and _____ .

c) Can you name three sports that don't use a ball?

_____ , _____ and _____ .

d) Can you name three team sports?

_____ , _____ and _____ .

3 **Read *Moving the Goalposts* on page 18 in the Student's Resource Book. Fill in the missing words to complete this paragraph about football.**

pitch	Football	goalposts	players	soccer	teams

_____ is a sport played on a _____. Two

_____ play against each other and try to kick the ball between the

_____. There are eleven _____ on each team. Another

name for football is _____.

4 **Choose the words to complete these two paragraphs.**

Moving the Goalposts is a _____ (sports centre / music centre) in

_____ (Ghana / Kenya). This centre teaches _____ (boys /

girls) how to play _____ (football / tennis). They practise ball skills and

working _____ (alone / together) as a team.

Many of the players play football without _____ (shoes / shirts / shorts),

_____ (because / but / so) they are happy to play the sport together.

This centre helps the girls make new _____ (meals / friends / bags) and

gives them more _____ (money / love / confidence). If they are very

good players, they can play against _____ (some / other) countries.

5 **Read this short paragraph. There are five spelling mistakes. Underline the mistakes and write the words correctly below.**

The girls love playing footbal and kiking the ball around on a fild. They work together as a teem and make new frends.

_____ _____ _____ _____ _____

39

6 **Read these paragraphs about Lionel Messi and fill in the missing words.**

> Argentina   famous   football   goal   medal   old
> records   sister   two   youngest   2008

Lionel Messi is one of the best _____ players in the world. He was born in _____ on the 24th of June, 1987. He has played for the Barcelona in the Spanish league and also for his country. Lionel has _____ brothers and one _____. He started playing soccer when he was four years _____.

When he first joined the Liga team, he broke two _____: he was the _____ footballer to play a league game, and also the youngest to score a league _____. In _____, he won an Olympic gold _____. He is one of the most _____ footballers in the world!

7 **Are these sentences about Lionel Messi true or false? If the sentence is false, rewrite it. Change the underlined word to make it true.**

Example: Lionel Messi is a famous <u>cricket</u> player.

False: Lionel Messi is a famous football player.

a) He was born in <u>Spain</u>.

_____: _____

b) He has three siblings – two <u>brothers</u> and one sister.

_____: _____

c) He was <u>five</u> years old when he started playing football.

_____: _____

d) He has won a <u>silver</u> medal at the Olympics.

_____: _____

8 These children are all watching the same football game. But they all show different feelings. Match the fan to the correct sentence.

a)   b)   c)   d)   e)

1 ☐ Fabio and Jerry are quite sad because their team is losing.

2 ☐ Ben is very angry because his team is losing.

3 ☐ Brian is really happy because his team is winning.

4 ☐ Sara is a little bored because her team isn't playing.

5 ☐ Marco can't concentrate because he is quite hungry.

9 Circle the correct answer. Use the picture of the thermometer to help you.

°C

really hot
very hot
hot
rather hot
quite hot
a little hot

a little cold
quite cold
rather cold
cold
very cold
really cold

a) Ice is (really cold / a little cold).

b) The Sun is (really hot / a little hot).

c) The water must be (quite hot / very hot) to make tea.

d) Polar bears live in places that are (a little cold / really cold).

e) You need to wear a jumper if it is (a little cold / rather hot).

f) In winter it is (cold / hot).

10 Complete these sentences with your own answers.

It is really fun to play _____.

It is rather exciting to watch _____.

It is a little noisy when _____.

It is very quiet when _____.

It is quite scary to hear _____.

It is really surprising to see _____.

11 **Listen to the article about mountain biking. Match the words with the correct meaning.**

balance •   • a narrow road or path

pedals •   • you push these with your feet to make a bicycle move

helmet •   • one time around a field or racecourse

a lap •   • to stay steady and not fall

track •   • difficult to climb up

obstacle •   • a hat that you use to protect your head

steep •   • something that makes it difficult for you to pass

12 **Circle all of the correct answers. Some questions have more than one answer.**

1 Mountain bikers ride

   a) on roads.   **b)** off roads.   **c)** up and down mountains.

2 What kind of obstacles must bikers get past?

   a) rocks   **b)** tree roots   **c)** cars

3 Mountain bikes have

   a) fat wheels.   **b)** thin wheels.   **c)** many gears.

4 What equipment do you need to mountain bike?

   a) a helmet   **b)** padded clothes   **c)** rope

13 **Complete these sentences with words from the box.**

| little dangerous   pretty simple   quite easy   rather bumpy   really difficult |

a) For many of us, riding a bicycle is _____ _____.

b) But after a while, it becomes _____ _____.

c) The path often has no clear track and can be _____

   _____.

d) Mountain biking can be a _____ _____, so you must wear a helmet.

e) The rules are _____ _____.

Week 2 Unusual sports

1 **Add the missing labels for the five senses to this diagram.**

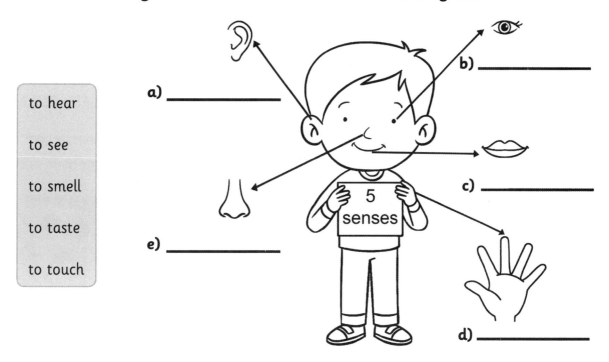

to hear

to see

to smell

to taste

to touch

a) _____

b) _____

c) _____

d) _____

e) _____

5 senses

2 **With your partner, read the words in the circles. Then answer these questions.**

What does each word mean?

Can you: See it?   Touch it?   Taste it?   Smell it?   Hear it?

ball

yellow

love

players

happiness

hate

friends

excitement

joy

anger

net

purple

court

uniforms

3 **Colour the circles with the words that are feelings.**

4 **Read both sentences in each pair below. Circle the sentence from each pair that has an abstract noun.**

> Abstract nouns are nouns that we cannot see, taste, touch, hear or smell.

a)   There are many soccer players.   There are many soccer rules.

b)   The stadium is full of excitement.   The stadium is full of people.

c)   Mario has a lot of talent.   Mario has a lot of friends.

d)   Andy is happy playing team sports.   Andy's happiness when he plays team sports is easy to see.

5 **Write the four abstract nouns below. Make a new sentence with each word.**

a)   _____ :   _____

b)   _____ :   _____

c)   _____ :   _____

d)   _____ :   _____

6 **Read these sentences. Circle the nouns you can touch, see, smell, hear or taste. Underline the nouns that you can't touch, see, smell, hear or taste.**

Example: She was given a (prize) for her talent.

a)   The ball hit the net.

b)   He dropped his phone with a crash.

c)   I was full of joy when my team won.

d)   Time is a great teacher.

e)   Sport is good for starting new friendships.

f)   I need to buy some milk and bread at the supermarket.

g)   My friends have a new kitten and it is full of energy.

7   Listen to *Cardboard tube duelling*. Circle the sentences you hear.

1   **a)** Cardboard duelling is sword fighting with cardboard tubes.

    b) Cardboard duelling is swordfish with cats and tubs.

2   **a)** Robins easily, an America, started the duel.

    b) Robert Easley, an American, started the duel.

3   **a)** He wanted ants to plague like children again and to be a little less severe.

    b) He wanted adults to play like children again and to be a little less serious.

4   **a)** The rules are very teasing and funny.

    b) The rules are very easy and fun.

5   **a)** Do not hit your opponent with your tube.

    b) Do not hurt the other person with your words.

6   **a)** Only hit your opponent's tummy.

    b) Only hit your opponent's tube.

7   **a)** Do not use your other hand to block or protect your tube.

    b) Do not use your left hand to blacken or provide a tube.

8   **a)** The aim is to break the other person's tube, so the last person with an unbroken tube is the winner.

    b) The aim is to bring the other person's tube, so the last person with an umbrella tube isn't the winner.

8   Draw a picture of a cardboard tube duel.

9   **Read the description of** *Belly flopping* **on page 20 in the Student's Resource Book. Then match the phrases to make complete sentences.**

This is the perfect sport for   •

• and land flat on your stomach and face.

A belly flop is when you jump into a pool   •

• at a belly flopping competition.

It makes a big splash and looks like lots of fun, but be careful   •

• as it can hurt.

Each person gets three dives   •

• people who are not good at diving.

10   **Answer these questions about belly flopping.**

a)   What is a belly flop?

_____

b)   How many dives does each person get at a belly flopping competition?

_____

c)   What three things can earn you points in a competition?

_____

_____

_____

d)   Would you like to enter a belly flopping competition? Why?

_____

_____

_____

The table below has nouns that you can see, touch, smell, taste or hear.

These are called **common nouns**.

It also has nouns that you cannot see, touch, smell, taste or hear.

These are called **abstract nouns**.

Many of these words are ideas or feelings.

11 **Can you find your way through the maze? Colour the words you cannot see, touch, smell, taste or hear. This will create a path from the start to the end. The first three have been done for you.**

START	manager	knowledge	childhood	mistake	yogurt
time	photograph	behaviour	badminton	habit	skateboarder
freedom	movement	membership	workbook	thought	friendship
shoulder	cinema	fast food	jeans	elevator	power
field	water bottle	imagination	education	worry	idea
hockey stick	timetable	advantage	rugby	bicycle	toothbrush
fisherman	luggage	decision	challenge	goalpost	laptop
mountain	juice	coach	future	energy	FINISH

12. **Choose five of the words you coloured in. Write a paragraph that includes them. You must write at least five sentences.**

_____

_____

_____

_____

_____

_____

Week 3 Fair play

1 **Write two objects needed to play these sports.**

Example: soccer We need <u>a soccer ball and a whistle.</u>

a) basketball We need _____.

b) table tennis We need _____.

c) hockey We need _____.

d) skateboarding We need _____.

2 **What are some important things you need to do every day? Use the words in the brackets to help you.**

(eat, breakfast) I need to _____.

(do, homework) I need to _____.

(brush, teeth) I need to _____.

(go, school) I need to _____.

3 **Listen to the story *If It Wasn't For Tom*. Complete these sentences using words in the box.**

finished	laughed	missed	wanted

a) Then Tom _____ and said I was useless.

b) He _____ every shot after that.

c) I _____ to show Mr Sim what I could do.

d) We _____ together, behind everyone else, but side by side.

4 **Look at the pictures. Read the sentences. Number the pictures in the correct order from 1 to 4.**

a) I kept running past Tom, huffing and puffing, his face red.

b) I missed the ball so many times
I was taken out of the team.

c) "Come on, Tom, you can do it!"
I said.

d) Then the new PE teacher came –
Mr Sim.

5 **Read the sentences. Number them in the correct order from 1 to 6.**

a) ☐ So Joe decided to help him.

b) ☐ The new PE teacher made Tom run.

c) ☐ Joe felt sorry for him.

d) ☐ Joe loved football and PE.

e) ☐ He really struggled to run.

f) ☐ But Tom always made fun of him.

6   **Choose the correct word to complete the polite questions.**

a)   (Will / Could) you help me, please?

b)   (Would / Could) you like a drink?

c)   Which cake (can / would) you like?

d)   (Could / Might) you shut the window?

e)   (Could / Would) I see the doctor?

f)   (Would / Will) you pass me my bag, please?

7   **Match the parts to make sentences to complete the conversation.**

Mika: For my holiday, I would like ●   ●   like to see tarsiers.

Jaryd: That would   ●   ●   animals would you like to see?

Mika: Where   ●   ●   be interesting.

Jaryd: I would   ●   ●   there to see the animals.

Mika: Why   ●   ●   to go to Japan.

Jaryd: I would go   ●   ●   go to the Philippines.

Mika: Which   ●   ●   would you go there?

Jaryd: I would   ●   ●   would you go?

8   **Look at pages 20–21 in the Student's Resource Book. Imagine you are inventing a new unusual sport. Answer these questions to help you.**

a)   What would you call your unusual sport?

I would call it _____

b)   Would people play the sport in teams or would they compete on their own?

People would _____

c)   How would people do or play your unusual sport?

People would _____

d)   What equipment would they need to play or do your unusual sport?

They _____

e)   How would people win?

To win, they _____

f)   Do you think your sport would be popular? Why?

_____

9 **Circle the best answer.**

1 Tomorrow is Rachel's birthday. You _____ her a present.

a) would buy **b)** need to buy

c) couldn't buy **d)** must buying

2 I have a terrible stomach ache.

a) You would eat more chocolate. **b)** You need to go to the nurse's office.

c) You could eat more chocolate. **d)** You mustn't go to the nurse's office.

3 I can't fall asleep.

a) You must turn off the light. **b)** You mustn't sleep.

c) You couldn't turn off the light. **d)** You would play a computer game.

10 **Use the words in the box to complete these sentences.**

> need to   must   mustn't

a) When you are riding your bicycle you _____ put on your helmet.
You _____ check that there is enough air in the tyres. You
_____ ride on very busy roads.

> mustn't   must   need to

b) When you play team sports you _____ have fun. You
_____ always follow the rules and listen to the referee. You
_____ say bad things to the other team or to your team-mates.

> mustn't   need to   have to

c) In basketball you _____ throw the ball into the basket to score a
goal. You can bounce the ball, but you _____ carry it or kick it. It
is a very fast game. If you get tired, you _____ take a break and
let someone else take your place.

11 **Read *Be a 'Good sport'* on page 23 in the Student's Resource Book. Complete these sentences using the words from the box.**

| angry | blame | mistakes | positive | practise | sad | say | skill |

It's not fun when someone is _____ when they lose. Sometimes we

feel _____ when we lose. But we mustn't get angry. Learning to lose

without getting angry is a _____. We need to _____ this

skill by doing these things:

● We need to _____ nice things, like "Well done!"

● We mustn't _____ other people if they make a mistake.

● We need to stay _____.

● We must learn from our _____.

12 **Draw a line to join the beginning of the sentence to the endings that make sense.**

If you want to be a good
sport, …

follow the rules

shout at the other players

blame other people when they
make mistakes

say nice things to the
other players

take turns

cheat

13 **Read about the unusual sports on pages 20–21 in the Student's Resource Book again. Write two sentences about the rules of those games. What must or mustn't you do?**

a) Belly flopping

_____

_____

b) Cheese rolling

_____

_____

c) Cardboard tube duelling

_____

_____

14 **Unscramble the words and rewrite these sentences.**

a) learn / game. / the rules / You / of the / need to

_____

b) need to / hard. / practise / You

_____

c) You / "good game!" / need to / the / say to / other team.

_____

d) play fair / You / need to / not cheat. / and

_____

e) cheer / need to / your team-mates. / for / You

_____

f) to play. / a chance / other people / give / need to / You

_____

15 **What must or mustn't you do at school? Colour the things you must do in blue. Colour the things you mustn't do in red.**

eat in class	do your homework	bring your books to school	use your phone in class
listen to the teacher	copy your friend's work	talk to your friend in a test	try your best

16 **Complete these sentences using 'must' or 'mustn't'.**

Example: In a library <u>you mustn't shout</u>.

a) After breakfast _____.

b) When you cross a road _____.

c) Before you go to bed _____.

d) When you swim _____.

e) When you are sick _____.

17 **Rewrite the underlined part of these questions and requests to make them polite. Use 'would' or 'could'.**

a) <u>Do you want to go</u> to the park? _____

b) <u>Can you bring</u> your ball with you? _____

c) <u>Can you close</u> the gate? _____

d) <u>Do you want</u> some chocolate? _____

e) <u>Can I have</u> a look at your comic? _____

18 **Complete the sentences with 'need to', 'must' or 'mustn't'.**

a) If you want to play sport, you _____ play fairly.

b) If you want to play fairly, you _____ cheat.

c) If you are in a team, you _____ say nice things to your team-mates.

d) If someone makes a mistake, you _____ blame them.

e) If you want to have fun, you _____ shout at other people.

Unit 4 Digital world

Week 1 The internet

1 **What can you do on the internet? Write one thing at the end of each line. Add more lines and ideas if you can.**

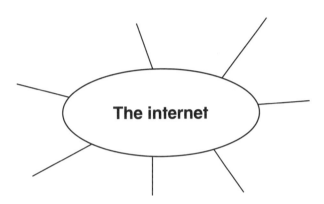

2 **Talk to your partner. Ask questions from this table. Cross off the questions when they have been asked and answered.**

Conversation cards: Let's talk about the internet!		
How often do you use the internet? Where do you use it?	Do you have an email address? Who do you email the most often?	What is your favourite website? Why do you like it?
Do you know anyone that does online shopping? What does he or she buy?	What do you use to message your friends? How many messages do you send every day?	Do you play games on the internet? How often do you play?
Do you watch 5 short videos on the internet? Describe a video that you really liked.	Do you download music or videos? Why or why not?	Do you use any social media networks? Describe the one you like the best and say why.

3 Match the action clouds to the correct computer words. There may be more than one correct word.

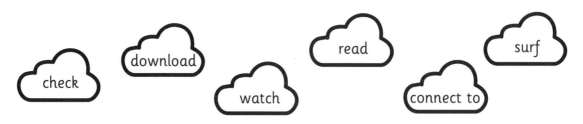

4 Read the poem *When Sarah Surfs the Internet* on page 24 in the Student's Resource Book. What does Sarah use the internet for?

_____

_____

_____

_____

_____

5 Answer these questions.

a) Who does Sarah chat with?

_____

b) What does she like to download?

_____

c) Do you think Sarah uses the internet to do work or to have fun? Why do you think so?

_____

d) Why do you think Sarah hasn't finished her homework?

_____

6   **Listen to *Things have changed.* Tick the correct answers.**

1   What does "Today, things are very different" mean?

  a) ☐ Computers have changed over the years.

  b) ☐ The internet has changed over the years.

  c) ☐ The way we do things has changed over the years.

2   How many people use the internet?

  a) ☐ Less than two thousand

  b) ☐ More than two billion

  c) ☐ Less than two billion

3   Which devices do people use to connect to the internet?

  a) ☐ PCs, laptops and smartphones

  b) ☐ Cell-phone reception, Wi-Fi and the internet

  c) ☐ Laptops, smartphones and Wi-Fi

4   How many hours of videos do people upload every minute?

  a) ☐ 60

  b) ☐ 72

  c) ☐ 80

5   What is bad about the internet?

  a) ☐ You can get information very quickly.

  b) ☐ You can buy music and download it.

  c) ☐ You can find a lot of information that is wrong.

6   Which sentence best describes the writer's opinion?

  a) ☐ The internet has changed our lives in good and bad ways.

  b) ☐ The internet has changed our lives in a good way.

  c) ☐ The internet has changed our lives in a bad way.

7   **Is the internet good or bad? Give one example to support your opinion.**

I think _____

_____.

8 **Complete this table to compare how people did things before and after the internet. If you are not sure, ask an adult to tell you how they did things before the internet.**

	Before the internet	Now
Find information for a school project	Went to the library to find information in books.	Search on the internet.
Communicate with a friend		
Buy music		
Keep up to date with news		
Watch a movie		

9 **Write about what life was like before the internet using the words in brackets to help you. Use 'I think', 'I believe', 'I am sure' or 'I am certain'.**

Example: (CD)   Before the internet, _I am sure that_ you had to _go to a music store to buy a CD_.

a) (library)   Before the internet, I _____ you had to

_____.

b) (photos)   Before the internet, I _____ you had to

_____.

c) (TV shows)   Before the internet, I _____ you had to

_____.

d) (news)   Before the internet, I _____ you had to

_____.

e) (talk to friends) _____

f) (maps) _____

g) (send a message) _____

10 **Read the sentences about the internet. Tick (✓) the advantages and cross (X) the disadvantages.**

a) ☐ You can find information for your homework.

b) ☐ You can get spam or a virus.

c) ☐ You can send a message quickly to someone far away.

d) ☐ You can meet other people who are interested in the same things as you.

e) ☐ Children can easily say or post unkind things about people at school.

f) ☐ Your parents' credit card number can be copied when they shop online.

g) ☐ You can share pictures of your life.

h) ☐ You can spend too much time online and get addicted.

i) ☐ People spend more time talking to strangers online than to their family in real life.

j) ☐ It is easy and fast to download things, like music.

k) ☐ You can get distracted, so you don't finish your homework.

l) ☐ You can share with friends on social media.

11 **Write the sentences above in the correct columns.**

Advantages of the internet:	Disadvantages of the internet:

12 **Listen to *The advantages and disadvantages of the internet* and add information to the table above.**

13 **Listen to Katrin and Ben giving their opinions about the internet. Discuss these questions in pairs.**

a) Does Ben think the internet is good or bad?

b) Why does he think this?

c) What does Katrin think?

d) Why does she think this?

14 **Now it is your turn to give an opinion. What do you think about the internet?**

_____

Why do you think so?

_____

_____

_____

15 **Write a complete paragraph about your opinion. Remember to give a main idea and write two or three details to support your opinion.**

_____

_____

_____

_____

_____

_____

Paragraph check: Change books with your partner.

Read his/her paragraph and check the following:

Is there a main idea?   Yes/No

Are there full stops at the end of every sentence?   Yes/No

Does the first letter of each new sentence start with a capital letter?   Yes/No

Are there details that support the opinion?   Yes/No

Week 2 The internet of things

1   **Look at this diagram. Tell your partner what it shows. Use the words in the box to help you.**

> camera   console   desk top computer   drone   fridge   games   kettle   laptop
> microwave   monitor   music system   smartphone   smartwatch   tablet

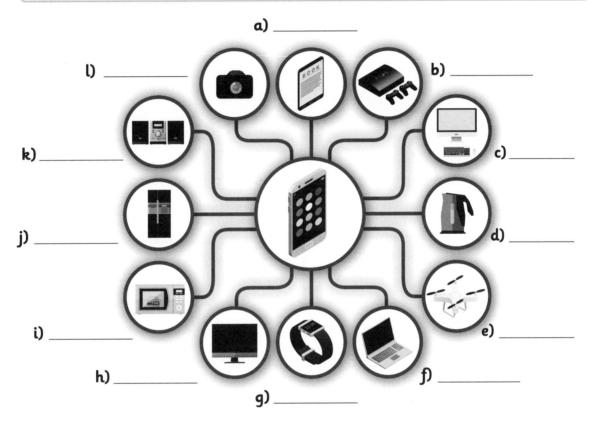

a) _____

b) _____

c) _____

d) _____

e) _____

f) _____

g) _____

h) _____

i) _____

j) _____

k) _____

l) _____

2   **Label the objects in the diagram. Use a dictionary to help you.**

3   **Write questions about the diagram. Swap books with your partner and answer each other's questions.**

Example: Question: *How might a smartwatch be useful?*

Answer: *It could measure your heart rate.*

a)   Question: _____

Answer: _____

b)   Question: _____

Answer: _____

4 Read *Let's connect* on page 25 in the Student's Resource Book. Match the words from the article (left column) to a word with a similar meaning (right column).

connect   •   • made

objects   •   • crazy

silly   •   • dream

little   •   • things

built   •   • join

control   •   • tiny

imagine   •   • request

order   •   • manage

5 Complete these sentences. Use words from the left column above.

There are many _____ that are _____ with _____ computers in them. It may sound _____, but in the future you may be able to talk to your fridge. If you need something your fridge can _____ some more. Your fridge will also be able to _____ the temperature so all your food stays nice and cold. _____ if all the electrical items in your house could _____ to the internet.

6 Read these sentences and decide whether they are a fact or an opinion. Write 'fact' or 'opinion'.

Example: <u>Opinion</u>   Cats are the best pets.

<u>Fact</u>   Cats can smell and hear better than humans.

a) _____   Computers make life easier.

b) _____   The internet helps computers, tablets and smartphones to share information.

c) _____   There are objects that have small computers in them.

d) _____   Some toothbrushes can connect to a smartphone.

e) _____   Brushing your teeth with a smart toothbrush is fun.

f) _____   I think smartwatches are too expensive.

g) _____   Some smartwatches have sensors that can measure your heart rate.

7 **Write a list of all the things a smartphone will do in the future.**

- It will open and close my curtains.
- It will tell me when my shower is the right temperature.
- It will _____.
- It will _____.
- _____
- _____
- _____
- _____

8 **Listen to the conversation between Sofia and Raul. Discuss these questions with your partner.**

What are they talking about?   Who thinks there will be robots in the future?

Which examples does Sofia mention?   Who will clean the house?

9 **Complete this conversation. Add punctuation to the last two sentences.**

Sofia: What do you _____ will happen in the future?

Raul: I'm not _____, but I _____ that every house will

have a robot.

Sofia: A robot! Why do you _____ so?

Raul: Because robots are useful and they can clean your house for you. I can

_____ you don't agree. What do you _____ will

happen in the future?

Sofia: Oh, I partly agree. I _____ there will be robots, but I

_____ they will be inside our appliances, like the fridge or

the TV.

Raul: What do you mean?

Sofia: A robot is a big computer, right?

Raul: Yes, I _____ so.

Sofia: Well, I _____ that things like your fridge and TV will have a
computer inside them and they will learn what you like and don't like.

Raul: Like your best friend?

Sofia: Yes, exactly!

Raul: So, who will clean the house

Sofia: I _____ that you will need to clean the house yourself

10 **Use the topic to complete the sentences. Choose your own topic for the
last sentences.**

Example: Paris

I am sure that _Paris is the capital of France._

I believe that _Paris is the most interesting city in the world._

a) Oranges

I am certain that _____.

I think that _____.

b) School

My parents know that _____.

My parents believe that _____.

c) _____

My best friend knows that _____.

My best friend hopes that _____.

11 **Choose the best word to complete these sentences.**

a) My sister _____ (know / hopes) that she will get a new bicycle for her birthday.

b) I _____ (thinks / hope) that I will pass my test because I studied hard.

c) Sofia _____ (believes / knows) that machines will learn what you like and don't like.

d) Raul _____ (know / hopes) that a robot will clean the house for him.

12 **What will happen in the future? Complete these sentences.**

a) Some of my friends think _____.

b) I am sure _____.

c) I believe _____.

d) I hope _____.

e) I am certain _____.

f) My parents know _____.

13 **Read the sentences and write the word that fits best.**

a) I _____ (know / think) that computers are very useful.

b) I _____ (know / think) that vegetables are good for my health.

c) My parents _____ (know / think) that I work hard at school.

d) Everyone _____ (knows / thinks) that the Moon is not made of cheese.

e) Many people _____ (know / think) that football is the best sport in the world.

Week 3 Smart devices

1 **Match the word to the correct meaning.**

notification   To shake with small, quick movements.

complain   A computer program.

argument   A group of things that are similar in some way.

honest   Something that is not real, or does not exist in the real world.

nervous   An angry or a loud conversation in which people disagree

vibrate   with each other.

collection   Telling the truth.

software   Where there are many different types or kinds of things.

variety   To say that you are not happy or satisfied about something.

identity   To be worried or frightened about something that might happen.

imaginary   An announcement that pops up on your phone.

                      Each person has one. Who and what you are.

2 **Use the words from above to complete these sentences.**

You may need to add -s to the end of some words.

a) When I get a new message, my phone _____ even when I put it on silent mode.

b) My mum _____ that I spend more time playing games than doing my school work.

c) Sam feels _____ before every maths test.

d) There is a _____ of different food in our fridge, like fruit, cheese, vegetables and jam.

e) I need to download special _____ onto my phone so I can play the new game.

f) My best friend never tells a lie, she is very _____.

g) Spider-Man wears a mask, so no one knows his real _____.

h) He and his sister had a loud _____, because they both wanted the last chocolate.

i) The art museum in my city has a large _____ of old paintings.

j) In the game *Minecraft* you have to create an _____ city.

k) My phone sends me a _____ every morning, to tell me what the weather is going to be like.

3 **Read the clues and complete the crossword puzzle.**

Across

5. Many different kinds

6. To be worried

8. A disagreement

9. An announcement on your phone

10. A program on a computer

Down

1. Unreal

2. Truthful

3. To shake

4. A group of similar things

7. What identifies you

4 Read *Help! I can't put my smartphone away* on page 26 in the Student's Resource Book. Answer these questions.

a) Do you think smartphones are good or bad? Why?

_____

_____

b) Are there any places where you mustn't use a smartphone? Why?

_____

_____

c) What is the best smartphone? Why? Draw a picture of it.

_____

_____

5 Write the letter of the correct sentence under each picture.

a) I'm even on my phone when I eat.   **b)** I message my friends when I go to bed.

c) My phone helps me do my homework. **d)** I don't like being apart from my phone.

1 _____   2 _____   3 _____   4 _____

6 Answer these questions.

a) What does Saskia do when she gets into bed every night?

_____

b) What does Rachel do while she is eating?

_____

c) When does Marco feel nervous?

_____

d) How does Finn finish his homework quickly?

_____

7 Discuss these questions and give your opinion.

Does Saskia have a problem? Why?

Why don't Rachel's parents want her to use her phone at the dinner table?

Do you agree with Rachel's parents?

Do you think Marco has a problem? Why?

Is it okay to use your phone to help you do homework? Why?

8 Choose the correct word to complete this advice.

a) Saskia _____ (mustn't / needs) use her phone in bed.

b) She _____ (mustn't / needs to) put her phone on silent before she goes to sleep.

c) Rachel _____ (needs / must) listen to her parents.

d) The first person to check their phone at a dinner table _____ (needs / must) wash all the dishes.

e) Marco _____ (mustn't / needs to) carry his phone in his bag.

f) He _____ (mustn't / must) switch off the vibrate mode, so it doesn't distract him when he is working.

g) Finn (mustn't / needs) _____ use his phone to find all the answers.

h) He _____ (mustn't / needs) to use his brain and do some of his homework on his own.

9 **Listen to the talk *Apps*. Discuss these questions.**

What is an app?

Give examples of apps.

What must you do when you create an online identity or character?

Which games does the talk mention? Do you know any others?

10 **There are many different types of apps. Match the app to the correct category. There are three apps in each category.**

You may need to do some research to complete this activity.

calculator

Candy Crush

Netflix

CNN

notepad

lifestyle

entertainment

music

chess

games

fitness app

utility

cooking app

travel app

news

BBC

Minecraft

weather app   New York Times

11 Read these sentences. Underline the correct word.

a) This is my friend (who / where) uses that great music app.

b) He's the boy (who's / whose) smart device is so cool.

c) I have a smartwatch (when / which) records my heart rate.

d) This is the place (who / where) we found the smartphone.

e) Is your phone the one (that / who) is yellow?

f) Do you remember (where / which) you left your tablet?

12 Look at the story *In the Game* on page 27 in the Student's Resource Book and discuss the questions.

a) Now look at this story.

b) What other events could happen behind Sara and Dan while they are absorbed in their game?

c) Draw the main events for your new idea in your notebook. Include speech bubbles for Sara and Dan.

Unit 5 School life

Week 1 Schools around the world

1 Label the pictures.

| bathroom | cafeteria | classroom | library | playground | ~~teacher~~ |
| tennis court | school building | sports hall | swimming pool |

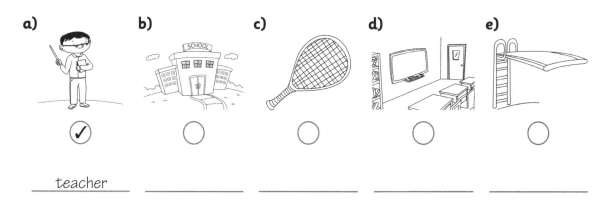

a) ✓
teacher

b) ⃝

c) ⃝

d) ⃝

e) ⃝

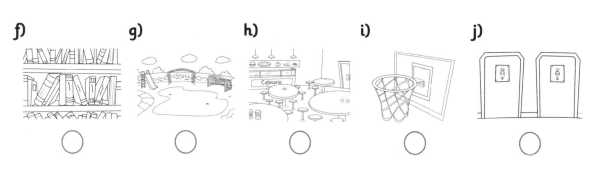

f) ⃝

g) ⃝

h) ⃝

i) ⃝

j) ⃝

2 Does your school have these places? Draw a tick ✓ in the circle if your school does and a cross ✗ if it doesn't.

3 What other things or places does your school have?

_____ _____ _____

_____ _____ _____

4   **Listen to Dev talk about his school. Fill in the missing words.**

at the entrance   behind   behind   downstairs   in front of
inside   next to   next to   outside   upstairs

Hello. My name is Dev and this is my school. There are about five hundred students, and we all wear a blue school uniform.

_____, there are many classrooms, two bathrooms and a library.

_____ the library, there is a computer room. The library is _____

the teacher's room.

_____, there are more classrooms. There is also a large cafeteria where

we eat our lunch. _____, there is a reception area. _____

this, is the headmaster's office.

_____, we have a large playground where we play at breaktime. The

playground is _____ the school. _____ the school, there is

a beautiful garden with many flowers. We are not allowed to play there. Our school

is raising money to build an indoor swimming pool and gym hall. They will be built

_____ the playground.

5   **Describe where places are at your school.**

_____

_____

_____

_____

_____

_____

_____

_____

_____

6 Look at the picture of Dev's classroom. Circle the correct words to complete these sentences.

a) The (book / boy) is (in / under) the chair.

b) The (plant / girl) is sitting (under / on) the chair.

c) The (poster / book) is (inside / on) the wall.

d) The (crayon / boy) is standing (next to / over) the bookshelf.

e) The (crayons / posters) are (under / in) the cup.

7 Make your own sentences. Use the words in brackets.

a) (in): _____

b) (on): _____

c) (under): _____

d) (next to): _____

e) (behind): _____

f) (in front of): _____

8 Check your sentences with a partner.

9 Read Dev's diary from his first day in Grade 5. He forgot to check his writing. Add the correct punctuation to complete Dev's diary.

dear diary   October 5th, 2019

today was my first day back at school wow i cant

believe i am already in grade 5 i am sad my summer

holidays are over but excited to see my friends again

i played soccer during lunch with arun and mao i like

them very much i hope they will become my new best

friends my new teacher is very funny he made us laugh

all day he gave us lots of homework today was a good

day will every day this year be good i hope so from dev

You can add:

capital letters

. full stops / periods

, commas

! exclamation marks

? question marks

' apostrophes

10 Imagine you have spent the day at one of the schools you read about. Write a diary entry about your day. Describe what you saw, what you did and how you felt.

Check the following:

☐ It includes the date.

☐ It includes the place.

☐ I wrote in the past tense.

☐ I checked my spelling.

☐ I checked my punctuation.

11   **Read about these unusual journeys to school.**

In many countries where people live on small islands, or next to large lakes, learners travel to school by boat.

In some places, like in areas of the Philippines, some children don't have boats. They float across the water on inflated tyre tubes or homemade rafts.

In a small village in Colombia, some children have to cross a deep valley to get to school. They travel by zipline to cross over the Negro River every day. It is more than 800 m long.

One of the most dangerous walks to school is in Pili, China. The learners travel 200 km on foot to reach their boarding school. This takes more than three days. They walk along narrow mountain paths, across frozen lakes and over dangerous bridges.

Some northern Russian villagers are nomadic. This means that they move their home a few times a year. The children of these families need to attend school in a town far from their homes. They go to boarding school by helicopter.

12   **Circle the word 'by' in the information above. How many times is the word used?**

_____

13   **Match the phrases to complete these sentences.**

In Colombia, some village children travel to school   by inflated tyre tubes.

In Russia, some nomadic children travel to school   by boat.

In the Philippines, some children travel to school   by helicopter.

In a small Chinese village, some children travel over 200 km   by zipline.

If your school is across the lake, you need to travel there   on foot.

14 **Answer these questions.**

a) How do you travel to school?

_____

b) How do you like to travel?

_____

c) How does your best friend travel to school?

_____

d) How do your parents travel to work?

_____

15 **Answer these questions in full sentences. Use the word in brackets and 'by' in each answer.**

Example: How does Tobias travel to school? (bus)

Tobias travels to school by bus.

a) How does Miguel travel to work? (train)

_____

b) How does Katarina travel to Germany? (aeroplane)

_____

c) How does Leo go to the Moon? (spaceship)

_____

d) How does Mary go to the library? (bicycle)

_____

16 **Read *Different schools* on pages 28–29 in the Student's Resource Book. Then, read these clues and write the answers in the puzzle.**

All the answers are in the text.

		¹c	l	a	s	s	r	o	o	m
					2					
		3								
					4					
5										
6										
7										
	8									
9										
10										

1. A room with chairs, desks and a teacher.

2. In India, some children go to school at a _____ station.

3. In Bangladesh, some children go to school on a _____.

4. At Brightworks, they believe the best way to learn is by _____ it yourself.

5. Travelling helps students learn about different cultures and _____.

6. _____ buildings differ from school to school.

7. Most learners study English, maths and _____.

8. At Brightworks, _____ can help you if you get stuck.

9. Another name for students.

10. Travelling school students visit a different _____ every semester.

What is the mystery word? _____

Week 2 Study methods

1 **Read *Study tips and tricks* on pages 30–31 in the Student's Resource Book. List the six study tips.**

a) _____   b) _____

c) _____   d) _____

e) _____   f) _____

2 **Answer these questions.**

a) Which study tips do you already use?

_____

b) Which study tips are new to you?

_____

_____

c) Which study tip(s) will you try to use for your next test?

_____

_____

d) Why?

_____

_____

3 **Mnemonics can be useful to help you remember how to spell difficult words. Choose a word from the box and make your own mnemonic.**

| enough | separate | pleasure | mathematics | environment | bought |

For example:

Rhythm

Rhythm Helps Your
Two Hips Move.

4 Read these sentences. Every sentence has at least two verbs. Circle all the verbs. If a verb is spelled incorrectly, rewrite it correctly on the line.

> When we talk about things we like / dislike, we often use verb + *ing*.
>
> When we talk about things we want or need, we often use *to* + verb

Example: Mia wants to sing and to laaf when she is happy. *laugh*

a) Carlos likes sleeping in the sunshine and dreeming about horses. _____

b) Carlos needs to sleep eight hours every night and to giv his body time to rest.

_____

c) Zara prefers swiming or playing in the sea on sunny days. _____

d) My sister wants to swam after school and to play with her friends. _____

e) I love jamping high while I am dancing to loud music. _____

f) When my mum is cooking, she loves lissening to the radio. _____

g) I want to sea the old city of Angkor Wat in Cambodia. _____

5 Read these sentences about Adelia and May. Write the correct form of the verb in brackets to complete the short stories

a) Adelia and her brother dislike _____ (go) to the shops with their mum. They prefer _____ (play) outside with their friends. But they are not allowed _____ (play) outside when their mum is not home. So, after shopping, Adelia and her brother can't wait _____ (go) outside to play!

b) Mei loves _____ (shop) with her mum. She wants _____ (visit) every shop in the world! Mostly, she enjoys _____ (see) all the different things for sale. Mei wants _____ (buy) everything.

6 Choose four of the verbs from the box. Write your own sentences using these verbs. Circle the verb pair as shown below.

be allowed dislike enjoy love need prefer can't wait want

Example: *be allowed: We are not allowed to talk when the teacher is talking.*

a) _____ : _____

b) _____ : _____

c) _____ : _____

d) _____ : _____

7 **Read this paragraph. Correct all the spelling and punctuation mistakes.**

all humens are diffarent We like different foods? different clothes, different activaties. we even like to learn in different ways, Some people like to learn by looking at things. Some people like, to learn by listening to things. Some peeple like to learn by doing things? How do yoo like to learn.

8 **What type of learner are you? Answer these questions. Circle the answers that suit you best.**

1 I like lessons when
  a) the teacher speaks and we sit and listen.
  b) we get to use our bodies to do actions in class.
  c) we have something to look at, like a video or presentation.

2 I often
  a) doodle or draw small pictures in my free time.
  b) hum or sing to myself.
  c) fiddle with things, like a pen or paperclip.

3 When learning something new, I like
  a) to have someone explain it to me.
  b) to have someone show me how to do it.
  c) to experience the real thing.

4 I would rather
  a) go outside and play.
  b) sit and watch my favourite show on TV.
  c) listen to my favourite music.

5 I get distracted in class if I
  a) see something happening outside.
  b) have to sit still for a long time.
  c) hear something happening outside.

6 Out of these three jobs, I would prefer to be
  a) a furniture maker.
  b) a designer.
  c) a radio DJ.

7 I like teachers who
  a) explain things to us.
  b) get us to do activities in class.
  c) use pictures to show things to us.

8 When I need to work with a story in class, I prefer
  a) to listen to the story.
  b) to read the story as a comic.
  c) to act out the story in a group.

9 **Circle your answers from the quiz in this table. Add up the total for each row.**

	1	2	3	4	5	6	7	8	Total
VISUAL LEARNER	c)	a)	b)	b)	a)	b)	c)	b)	
AUDITORY LEARNER	a)	b)	a)	c)	b)	c)	a)	a)	
KINAESTHETIC LEARNER	b)	c)	c)	a)	c)	a)	b)	c)	

I am mostly a _____.

10 **Make a mind map.**

a) Choose one person from your family. Write his or her name in the middle of the mind map.

b) Add lines with sub-topics.

Here are some ideas, but you can add anything.

- Basic information (full name, age, nationality, birthday)
- Things they like
- Things they don't like
- Interests and hobbies

c) Fill in all the details.

d) Use coloured pencils and make it look great.

e) Present your mind map to your group.

Week 3 School stories

1   **Read *Harry the Clever Spider at School* on pages 32–34 in the Student's Resource Book. Answer these questions in full sentences.**

a)   Who was Harry's owner?

_____

b)   Why did Harry go to school?

_____

c)   What pet did Joanna bring to school?

_____

d)   What was Simon's minibeast?

_____

e)   Why did Miss Bradley want the minibeasts to stay in their jars and boxes?

_____

f)   Was this the first time Miss Bradley had lost her glasses?

_____

g)   What did Miss Bradley want the learners to do with their minibeasts?

_____

h)   Who found Miss Bradley's glasses?

_____

i)   Where were her glasses?

_____

j)   What did Clare say about Harry?

_____

2   **Draw a picture of Harry the spider. Complete the sentence with three words that describe him.**

I think Harry the spider is

_____,

_____ and

_____.

3 Draw a minibeast you would take to school. Describe it.

_____

_____

_____

4 Read the story *Harry the Clever Spider at School* on pages 32–34 in the Student's Resource Book. Find words in the story that have a similar meaning to:

Words that have similar meanings are called synonyms.

a) insects: _____

b) intelligent: _____

c) big: _____

d) arachnid: _____

e) furry: _____

f) spectacles: _____

g) beautiful: _____

h) container: _____

i) shouted: _____

j) sketch: _____

5 Find words in the story that have the opposite meaning to:

Words that have opposite meanings are called antonyms.

a) small: _____

b) full: _____

c) off: _____

d) everyone: _____

e) white: _____

f) happy: _____

g) down: _____

h) in front: _____

i) outside: _____

j) whispered: _____

6 **Read these sentences. If the sentence is true, write 'True' and rewrite the sentence. If the sentence is false, write 'False' and rewrite the sentence, correcting the underlined word(s).**

Example: Harry was Clare's pet <u>beetle</u>.

False: Harry was Clare's pet spider.

a) Harry was very <u>clever</u>.

_____: _____

b) <u>Miss Bradley</u> was the class teacher.

_____: _____

c) The learners were learning about <u>wild animals</u> at school.

_____: _____

d) Miss Bradley lost her <u>bag</u>.

_____: _____

e) Harry was hiding <u>in the corner</u> of the box so no one could see him.

_____: _____

f) <u>Nobody</u> was helping Miss Bradley look for her glasses except Clare.

_____: _____

g) <u>Harry</u> found Miss Bradley's glasses.

_____: _____

h) Miss Bradley was <u>angry</u> that Harry had got out of his box.

_____: _____

i) Harry found the glasses behind the <u>door</u>.

_____: _____

7 Read this paragraph about 'Show and tell'. Circle all the missing capital letters.

show and tell

in america, show and tell is a classroom activity. learners bring an interesting thing from home to show their classmates. they can bring anything: a good book, a fun toy, an old shoe or sometimes even a cute pet. learners stand in front of their class and talk about their special object.

8 Underline the six adjectives in the paragraph above.

9 Use four of the underlined adjectives to complete these sentences.

a) This _____ computer was made in America, in 1995.

b) My cat was very _____ when she was a kitten.

c) I kept all my _____ things in a drawer, which I always locked.

d) We went on holiday and saw many _____ places.

10 Write sentences using the two adjectives you didn't use.

_____

_____

11 Read the paragraph about Fabio and then write the correct form of the verb in brackets to complete the sentences.

Fabio loved _____ (bring) things from home to show his class. He

wanted _____ (bring) his pet spider, but Fabio's teacher said he was not

allowed _____ (bring) his spider to school. She said the only thing she

wanted him _____ (bring) was his smile.

12 **Read the story *Harry the Clever Spider at School* on pages 32–34 in the Student's Resource Book. Fill in the missing words.**

Last week at school, Clare's class _____ (learn) about minibeasts. Clare wanted to show her friends her pet spider, Harry. She put him in a box for the journey to school. When Clare got to school, Harry _____ (hide) in the corner of his box. He jumped out as soon as Clare opened the lid. Clare shouted for help, but her teacher _____ (not listen) because she _____ (look) for her glasses. While all the children _____ (look) for Miss Bradley's glasses, Clare _____ (try) to find Harry. When she finally found him, he _____ (bungee jump) from the ceiling. He jumped down behind the cupboard and found Miss Bradley's glasses. She was very happy to be able to see again!

13 **Circle the correct verb in brackets to complete the sentences.**

a) I (watched / was watching) TV when she called.

b) She was writing her next blog when the phone (rang / was ringing).

c) While we (had / were having) the picnic, it started to rain.

d) What were you (did / doing) when the earthquake (started / starting)?

e) I (listened / was listening) to music, so I (didn't hear / wasn't hearing) the phone ring.

f) Last night, someone (stole / was stealing) Jackie's car, while he (slept / was sleeping).

14 **What happened at school yesterday? Write a paragraph describing some of the things you did. Include what you were doing when something else happened. For example, what were you doing when the bell rang for break time?**

_____

_____

_____

_____

_____

15 **Create a comic strip about *Harry the Clever Spider at School*. Draw the pictures and add speech bubbles.**

Harry the Clever Spider Goes to School

Title: _____   Author: _____

Unit 6 Communication

Week 1 The art of language

1 **Is this communication? Circle the answer.**

1 Two people talking

    a) Yes   **b)** No

2 Smiling

    a) Yes   **b)** No

3 Writing a letter

    a) Yes   **b)** No

4 Sleeping

    a) Yes   **b)** No

5 Waving goodbye

    a) Yes   **b)** No

Did you know?

When we are awake, we spend about 70% of our time communicating with other people.

We can divide communication into five groups: reading, writing, listening, speaking and body language.

2 **Write different examples of each of these ways of communicating.**

READING	WRITING

LISTENING	SPEAKING
listening to music	*making a phone call*

BODY LANGUAGE

3 **The average Grade 5 English student reads aloud at a rate of about 130 words per minute. The paragraph below is exactly 130 words. Can you read it aloud in a minute?**

I will go to India this spring. I haven't been to India before. In fact, I haven't been to any other country before. I am very excited. I haven't even flown in an aeroplane. I feel a little nervous about this. My dad says we will be safe and my mum says it will even be fun. My brother told me the food is good and you can watch many movies. I love movies! There are two things I want to do in India. I want to see the Taj Mahal. I have seen beautiful buildings, but I think this is the most beautiful in the world. I also want to taste real Indian curry. I have eaten spicy food before, but I think it will be better in India!

Answer these questions about the paragraph.

a) Where will the writer fly to? _____

b) Has she been there before? _____

c) What does she feel nervous about? Why?

She feels nervous about _____ because
_____.

d) What does she want to do in this country? Why?

_____

She wants to _____ because
_____.

She also wants to _____ because
_____.

4 **Read the paragraph three times. Time yourself each time.**

a) How long did it take you to read 130 words?

First reading: _____ Second reading: _____
Third reading: _____

b) Ask five learners how long it took them to read 130 words.

c) Did you get faster each time? _____

d) What is your comfortable speed? _____

e) What is your fastest speed? _____

5 **Read *Mojo and Weeza and the Funny Thing* on page 36 in the Student's Resource Book. Fill in the missing words in this summary of the story.**

Mojo and Weeza found an _____, but they didn't know what it was. First, they thought it was a _____, but _____ _____ _____. Next, they thought it was a _____, but it didn't _____ _____. Then Mojo thought it was a _____, but when he jumped out of the tree, it didn't work. Then, Weeza thought it was a _____, but it was _____ _____. Finally, it started raining. Mojo said, "_____ _____ _____ _____ _____!" In the end, they decided it was a _____.

6 **Work with a partner. Look at the objects below. Can you think of two different ways you can use them? Be creative!**

a book	To sit on.	To store secret things in.
a box	_____ _____ _____	_____ _____ _____
a table	_____ _____ _____	_____ _____ _____
a cup	_____ _____ _____	_____ _____ _____

7   **Imagine you have a pen pal. Fill in this information about your pen pal.**

Name: _____

Girl/Boy: _____ Age: _____

Country: _____

Hobbies: _____

8   **Write a letter to a pen pal. Write about what you have done this week. Ask them questions about their life.**

Remember: connectives can help to make your ideas flow.

_____

_____

_____

_____

_____

_____

_____

_____

_____

_____

_____

9 **Read this text message. Write a reply. Use the box to help you.**

Hey!

hw r u? ms u! gd hols? 😎

hope u're gr8!

It's my bday 2mrw 🔺, but I wanna cu 2d. U free b4 6pm 4 t? ☕

Cn meet @ Cafe Blue.

Lmk! hope 2 c u l8r! 😊

xoxo

_____

_____

_____

_____

_____

2	to/too	4	for	b4	before	luv/lv	love
l8r	later	@	at	gr8	great	lol	laugh out loud
r	are	u	you	c	see	b	be
coz/cz	because	lmk	let me know	pls/plz	please		

10 **Number the conversation lines in the correct order from 1 to 10.**

	Victor:	That's fantastic!
	Victor:	Really? Wow! Where have you been?
	Victor:	Oh really, what have you done since I saw you last?
	Victor:	Hi, Ellen! I haven't seen you for ages! What have you been up to?
	Victor:	That's incredible! I haven't visited any of those places.
	Ellen:	Yes, it has been a long time. I've been busy.
	Ellen:	Perhaps you need to learn photography too. It's a great way to travel!
	Ellen:	Yes, absolutely fantastic! I've travelled all around the world to take pictures.
	Ellen:	This month, I have been to Paris, London and New York. Next month, I'm going to Singapore and Tokyo.
	Ellen:	Well, I have just started a new job as a fashion photographer.

11 **Listen to your teacher carefully. Fill in the missing words.**

| apple | box | carrot | fire | flower | fork | mug |

Look at this grid. In the first block, there is a mouse. To the right of the mouse, there is a _____. Underneath the _____, is a _____. Two blocks below the _____ is a _____. To the left of the _____ is a _____. In the bottom, right block, there is an _____. Above the apple is a _____. Two blocks to the left of the _____ is a _____. This _____ is two blocks below the mouse.

12 **Listen to your teacher carefully. Draw the things in your grid in the correct place.**

13 **Listen to the description of the *Strange Thing*. Write five facts about it.**

The *Strange Thing*

_____

_____

_____

_____

_____

What do you think the *Strange Thing* can do?

Why do you think it is always happy?

14 **Draw your own *Strange Thing*. Write five things about the thing.**

15 **Listen to your partner's description. Write the five points. Draw their *Strange Thing* without looking at their picture.**

Does your picture match their *Strange Thing*?

Week 2 Secret codes and sign language

1 Look at this grid. Make as many words as you can.

M	R	S
Y	E	E
I	S	T

_____ _____ _____

_____ _____ _____

_____ _____ _____

a) How many words can you make using these letters? _____

b) Can you make a word using all nine letters? _____

2 Circle all the verbs in this paragraph.

Rob was a kid detective. He loved to solve mysteries. Every day, Rob walked home from school. He always carried a magnifying glass in his pocket. He also held a notepad and a pencil in his hand. He wrote about everything he saw. He noticed many interesting things. He thought a lot about puzzles and he sang while he walked. Rob was a super kid detective!

3 Look at this wordsearch.

a) Find the eight past forms in this wordsearch.

> loved   walked   carried   held   wrote   noticed   thought   sang

L _ _ _ _

W _ _ _ _ _

C _ _ _ _ _ _

H _ _ _

W _ _ _ _

N _ _ _ _ _ _

T _ _ _ _ _ _

S _ _ _

W	E	C	A	R	R	I	E	D	L	L
D	O	N	E	S	A	N	G	F	O	R
T	H	O	U	G	H	T	S	O	L	V
H	I	N	G	N	O	T	I	C	E	D
E	L	O	V	E	D	W	R	O	T	E
L	T	H	E	M	Y	S	T	E	R	Y
D	W	A	L	K	E	D	C	O	D	E

b) Find the secret sentence in the unused letters.

W _ _ _ _ _ _ _ _ _ _ _ _ _ _ _ _ _ _ _ _ _ _ _ _ _ _ _ _ _ _ _ !

4 **Crack this code to reveal a sentence.**

A	B	C	D	E	F	G	H	I	J	K	L	M
2	12	11	20	4	15	19	5	8	14	25	7	16
N	O	P	Q	R	S	T	U	V	W	X	Y	Z
9	22	10	21	3	13	6	1	23	18	26	24	17

7 2 13 6   18 4 4 25,   8   13 2 6   2 9 20   20 3 4 18

_ _ _ _   _ _ _ _   _   _ _ _   _ _ _   _ _ _ _

15 22 3   6 18 22   5 22 1 3 13.

_ _ _   _ _ _   _ _ _ _ _

6 5 4 9,   8   13 2 9 19   18 5 8 7 4   8   12 1 8 7 6   2

_ _ _ _   _   _ _ _ _   _ _ _ _ _   _   _ _ _ _ _   _

12 7 22 11 25   6 22 18 4 3.

_ _ _ _ _   _ _ _ _ _

5 **Complete these sentences.**

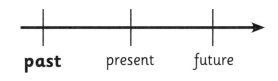

past   present   future

> built   chased   drew   listened   loved   sang   sat   studied   watched

a) The Egyptians _____ the pyramids thousands of years ago.

b) When I was in Grade 2, I _____ playing dodge ball.

c) Craig _____ and _____ the sunset last night.

d) Julie's dog _____ the ball in the park.

e) I _____ very hard for my science exam.

f) Lucy _____ to her favourite song on the radio.

g) My friends _____ 'Happy Birthday' to me last week.

h) The artist _____ a beautiful picture yesterday.

6 **Tell your partner or group a story. Use as many of the verbs in the box as possible. Remember to use connectives to help your story flow.**

7 **Change the verbs below into the past simple form.**

Example: listen ⇨ *listened*

a) chase ⇨ _____   **b)** sit ⇨ _____

c) love ⇨ _____   **d)** sing ⇨ _____

e) draw ⇨ _____   **f)** watch ⇨ _____

g) study ⇨ _____   **h)** build ⇨ _____

8 **Write the correct word to complete these paragraphs.**

Andrew _____ (love / loved) unsolved mysteries of the world! How _____ (do / did) the Egyptians _____ (build / built) the pyramids? Does the Loch Ness Monster _____ (exist / existed)? Why have people _____ (disappear / disappeared) in the Bermuda triangle? _____ (Is / Was) it real? These were questions Andrew _____ (think / thought) about all the time.

Andrew also _____ (enjoy / enjoyed) trying to _____ (solve / solved) small mysteries. Who _____ (eat / ate) his lunch yesterday? What would his mum _____ (cook / cooked) for dinner? What _____ (is / was) his brother doing? Sometimes he and his friends _____ (write / wrote) secret messages to each other. They _____ (write / wrote) using different mystery codes so that no one could _____ (solve / solved) their coded messages.

9 **Look at the different codes on pages 38–39 of your Student's Resource Book. Choose one of them and write instructions for someone to use it.**

_____

_____

_____

_____

10 **Look at the words in the table. Identify the root word and find other words that can be made from the root word. The first two words have been done for you.**

Word	Root word	Other words
interesting	*interest*	*interested, interestingly, uninteresting, uninterested, uninterestingly, disinterest, disinterested*
reheat	*heat*	*heated, heating, heater, preheat, overheat*
amazement		
amused		
alone		
useless		
happiness		
friendship		

11 **What do the words you have found mean? Choose two of the root words. Write two sentences using other words made from the root words.**

Example: Root word: <u>interest</u>

       1: <u>The codes in this unit are very interesting.</u>

       2: <u>We were most interested in the Loch Ness Monster.</u>

Root word: _____

1: _____

2: _____

Root word: _____

1: _____

2: _____

12 Look at these puzzles and solve them. Use the phrases in the box to help you.

All around the world   Just between you and me   Backpack
Once in a blue moon   Thinking outside the box   Look both ways
I understand   Forgive and forget   Looking good

ʞOO⅃ LOOK	GIVE GIVE GIVE GIVE GET GET GET GET	Pack
B1L1U1E M10101N	ALL ALL WORLD ALL ALL	thinking
YOU J U S T ME	stand ————— I	GOOD

13 Sometimes, English phrases have meanings that aren't obvious. We call these phrases 'idioms'. Can you match the idiom to its meaning?

1   Just between you and me.   **a)**   To be creative and think differently.

2   Once in a blue moon.   **b)**   When something is a secret.

3   Thinking outside the box.   **c)**   Very, very rarely (not often).

Week 3 Speaking in front of a crowd

1 **Read *Marvellous Milly Makes Her First Speech* on pages 40–41 in the Student's Resource Book. Answer these questions.**

a) Where is Milly from? _____

b) Where has Milly moved to? _____

c) What does Milly's teacher ask her to do?

_____

d) How does Milly feel about making a speech? _____

e) At first, what does Milly's voice sound like? _____

2 **Answer these questions.**

a) Have you ever moved to another country?   Yes/No

b) If yes, how did you feel? _____

c) Have you ever made a speech?   Yes/No

d) If yes, how did you feel? _____

3 **List the things which Milly talks about.**

_____

4 **Summarise *Marvellous Milly Makes Her First Speech* in five sentences.**

_____

_____

_____

_____

5 **Read this paragraph.**

Kamil has a big family. He has a mother, Azima. She has seen the Great Wall of China, but she hasn't visited China since then. Kamil's father is Jabir. Jabir has worked as a carpenter for twenty years. Kamil's older brother is called Abdel. He has written a book about ships. The next oldest is Kamil's sister, Rafa. Rafa has joined a choir to practise singing. Kamil is the third oldest child. He has saved money to buy a remote-controlled car. He will be twelve years old next week. The youngest child is Sagira. Sagira has just learned how to walk.

6 **Answer these questions about Kamil's family.**

    a)   Who has seen The Great Wall of China? _____

    b)   Who has just learned to walk? _____

    c)   Who has joined a choir to practise singing? _____

    d)   Who has saved money to buy a toy car? _____

    e)   Who has worked in his job for twenty years? _____

    f)   Who has written a book about ships? _____

7 **Look again at the description of Kamil's family. Write the words from the text that give the answers to these questions.**

    a)   Has his mother been to China between when she saw the Great Wall and now?

    _____

    b)   Does his father have the same job now as 15 years ago?

    _____

8 Complete these questions and answer them. Try to use *since* and *for* in your answers.

Have you ever *seen* (see) a panda?	Have you ever *travelled* (travel) by aeroplane?	Have you ever _____ (fly) a kite?
Yes, I have seen a panda but not since I was young.	*No, because my family hasn't travelled by plane for years.*	_____ _____
Have you ever _____ (plant) a flower?	Have you ever _____ (hear) a fantastic song?	Have you ever _____ (eat) sushi?
_____ _____	_____ _____	_____ _____
Have you ever _____ (write) a letter?	Have you ever _____ (have) a pet?	Have you ever _____ (dance) with a friend?
_____ _____	_____ _____	_____ _____

9   **Choose the correct words to complete these paragraphs.**

Public speaking is when you _____ (stand / sit) up in front of a
_____ (crowd / pair) of _____ (animals / people) and make
a speech. Many people (felt / feel) nervous when they (have / must) to make a speech.
_____ (Sometimes / Anytimes) they speak softly or _____
(to / too) fast. Sometimes their hands shake or _____ (their / there)
knees tremble. Sometimes their face _____ (go / goes) red or they
_____ (can / can't) speak at all.

Other people love public _____ (speaking / speak). When they stand up
in front of a group of people they _____ (speaks / speak) slowly, clearly
and _____ (loud / loudly). They remember all their words. They use
expressive body language and _____ (are / is) very interesting. Public
speaking _____ (are / is) an important skill to learn.

10   **Write questions about public speaking. Then answer the questions.**

Have you ever _____?

_____

Have you ever _____?

_____

Have you ever _____?

_____

Have you ever _____?

_____

Have you ever _____?

_____

11   **Choose a paragraph from an English book that you enjoy. Practise
reading the paragraph aloud, then read it to your group.**

12 **Choose one of the topics below. Prepare a short speech about the topic.**

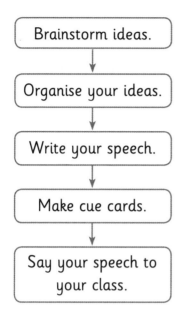

Brainstorm ideas.

↓

Organise your ideas.

↓

Write your speech.

↓

Make cue cards.

↓

Say your speech to your class.

Topic ideas

A little bit about me

My family

My favourite animal

My favourite hobby

Connectives and adverbs of sequence will help you organise your ideas.

Don't forget to check your spelling and punctuation!

_____

_____

_____

_____

_____

_____

_____

_____

_____

_____

_____

_____

Unit 7 Location and direction

Week 1 Modern-day treasure hunting

1   **Read about geocaching on page 42 in the Student's Resource Book. Answer these questions in your own words.**

a)   What is geocaching?

_____

b)   Where does geocaching happen?

_____

c)   How many treasures are hidden around the world?

_____

d)   How can you find a treasure?

First, _____.

Then, _____.

e)   What must you do when you find a treasure?

First, _____.

Then, _____.

2   **Follow these instructions.**

Underline the correct word in brackets.

Circle the missing capital letters.

Fill in the missing punctuation.

a)   a treasure is something that is very special to (I / you)

b)   do (you / it) have any special treasures

c)   maybe (they / you) have a favourite toy a secret diary or a piece of jewellery that (you / it) really love

d)   (this / these) is your treasure

e)   (someone / everything) might treasure (its / their) car

f) (nothing / somebody) might treasure a flower in their garden

g) almost (no one / somebody) treasures dust

h) almost (everyone / someone) treasures their family

i) what is (you / your) special treasure

3 **Write three things that you treasure.**

_____   _____   _____

4 **Draw your three treasures.**

Describe your treasures to your group and tell them why they are special.

5 **Answer these questions about geocaching with only one word. Use the first paragraph of the article on page 42 in the Student's Resource Book to help you.**

Example: What can you find?   _Anything!_

a) Who can play?   _____

b) When can you play?   _____

c) Where can you play?   _____

6 Draw lines to connect these words to create new words. Write the words below.

some ● ———————————— ● thing

any ●   ● one

every ●   ● where

no ●

a) *something* _____ _____

b) _____ _____ _____

c) _____ _____ _____

d) _____ _____ _____

7 Draw a line to connect the words that mean the same.

no one ●   ● somebody

someone ●   ● everybody

everyone ●   ● nobody

8 Complete these sentences using the words in the box.

| No one | Someone | Everyone |

a) _____ in our class needs food and water to live.

b) _____ in our class has one hundred sisters.

c) _____ in our class is the fastest runner.

9 Complete these sentences using the words in the box.

| Nobody | Somebody | Everybody |

a) _____ in the world can run as fast as a cheetah.

b) _____ in the world breathes air.

c) _____ in the world is taller than me.

10 Write your own sentences, using the word given.

a) nothing: _____

b) something: _____

c) everything: _____

d) nowhere: _____

e) somewhere: _____

f) everywhere: _____

11 Read the *The Amazing Race* on page 42 in the Student's Resource Book. Label the forms of transport. Draw a line to connect them to 'sea', 'land' or 'air'.

a) _____ **b)** _____ **c)** _____

d) _____ **e)** _____ **f)** _____

g) _____ **h)** _____ **i)** _____

j) _____ **k)** _____

| sea | land | air |

12   Fill in the prepositions to complete this text about *The Amazing Race*.

The Amazing Race is a game show _____ television. _____

the show, teams race _____ the world _____ treasure

hunts. The teams travel _____ different places all over the world to

find treasure. They race _____ land, _____ water and

_____ the air, using boats, helicopters and other vehicles.

13   Match the nouns to the prepositions. Some nouns can go with more than one preposition.

Prepositions	Nouns	
on	home	lunch time
by	foot	the sea
in	car	holiday
at	television	school
	the morning	hospital
	email	the countryside

Write the preposition and noun in the table.

on	by	in	at
on foot			

14   Read *Metal Detecting* on page 43 in the Student's Resource Book and then complete these sentences.

a)   People use metal detectors to _____.

b)   In 1977, a metal detector was used to _____.

c)   In 2007, a metal detector was used to _____.

d)   In 2012, a metal detector was used to _____.

15 **You are going to write a story in your notebook. Follow the steps in the flowchart to help you.**

Step 1: Think of a character to write about and talk to your partner.

Who are they?   What do they look like?

Where are they?   What will happen to them?

What are they doing?

↓

Step 2: Brainstorm ideas.

Title

| Beginning | Middle | Ending |

↓

Step 3: Think about how you can include some of these words:

something	someone	somewhere	nothing
anything	anyone	anywhere	no one
everything	everyone	everywhere	nowhere

↓

Step 4: Write a first draft in your notebook.

↓

Step 5: Read your draft aloud to yourself or to your partner.

Think about these things:

Does my story have a beginning, a middle and an ending?	Yes/No
Did I use capital letters correctly?	Yes/No
Is the spelling correct? (Use a dictionary to check.)	Yes/No
Is the punctuation correct?	Yes/No
Do the sentences make sense?	Yes/No

↓

Step 6: Write a final version of your story. Make the changes that you need to make. Add pictures.

16 **Complete these sentences with the correct form of the word in brackets.**

a) Did you meet _____ nice at the party?
(anyone / nowhere)

b) I've looked _____ for my keys, but I still can't find them.
(anywhere / everywhere)

c) Ouch! There's _____ in my eye.
(something / anything)

d) _____ likes friendly people.
(Everyone / No one)

e) _____ likes a mean person.
(Everyone / No one)

f) My bag is empty. There is _____ inside.
(something / nothing)

g) Our teacher is so kind. _____ loves her!
(everywhere / everyone)

h) Did you buy _____ from the shop?
(anything / somewhere)

i) I'm bored. I want _____ fun to do or _____ fun to
talk to.   (someone / something)   (someone / something)

j) _____ in the world has elephants that can fly.

(Anywhere / Nowhere)

17 **Complete and then answer these questions. Your answer must start
with 'To …'. Be creative.**

Example: Why do *people use Smartphones? To chat to their friends.*

a) Why does _____

b) Why did _____

c) Why did _____

d) Why do _____

Week 2 **Understanding maps**

1 **Read *What is a map?* on pages 44–45 in the Student's Resource Book. Use the article to help you label the following map features.**

Natural features:

a)    b) 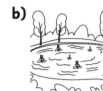   c)    d)    e)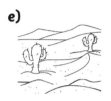

_____ _____ _____ _____ _____

Built features:

a) 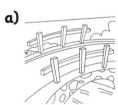   b) 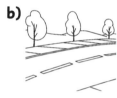   c)    d)    e)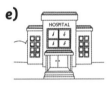

_____ _____ _____ _____ _____

2 **Complete these sentences about the article.**

a) A map is _____.

b) Maps can show large areas like _____ or _____.
   They can also show small areas in a city like _____ or
   _____.

c) Natural features you can see on a map: _____, _____
   and _____.

d) Built features you can see on a map: _____, _____
   and _____.

e) A person who draws maps is called a _____.

f) A long time ago, _____ would find out information about
   new places.

g) Now we use _____ and _____ to help
   us make maps.

3   **Look at this map. Tell your partner what you can see.**

My town

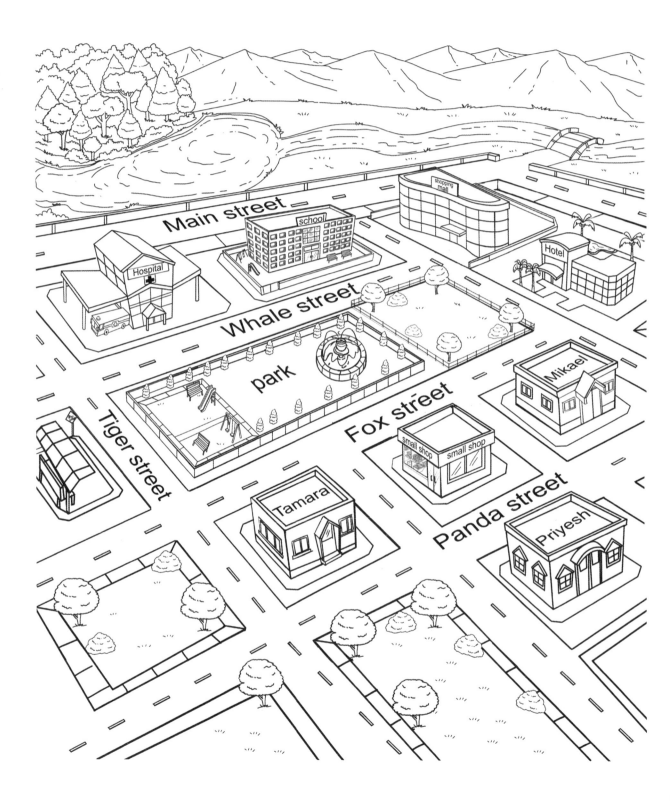

4 Look at the map on page 114. Tick (✓) the things you can see. Cross (✗) the things you cannot see.

☐ bicycle ☐ bridge ☐ car ☐ desert ☐ elephant

☐ house ☐ library ☐ mountain ☐ park ☐ police station

☐ road ☐ river ☐ shopping centre ☐ swimming pool ☐ zoo

5 Use the phrases in the box to complete these sentences. Each phrase can be used only once.

> across from   far from   in between   next to   on the corner of

a) The small shop is _____ Tamara's house and Mikael's house.

b) The hospital is _____ the park.

c) Priyesh's house is _____ the lake.

d) The hotel is _____ the shopping mall.

e) The park is _____ Whale Street and Tiger Street.

6 Look at the map on page 114. Choose the correct words to complete the conversation.

Ziad: Where does Tamara live?

Selina: (At / On) Panda Street.

Ziad: How do you get there (from / of) the hospital?

Selina: You go (out of / at) the hospital and go (across / along) Whale Street. Turn (down / by) Tiger Street. Go (past / into) the park and cross (over / of) Fox Street. Tamara's house is (in / of) the first block (on / in) the left (by / on) Panda Street.

Ziad: Thanks!

7 Practise similar conversations with a partner.

8   Read these conversations with a partner.

A: Excuse me, Ma'am, could you tell me how I get to the lake from here?

B: Go straight on, then turn right into Wellington Street.

A: Thank you.

A: Excuse me, Sir, how do I get to the hospital from here?

B: Turn left down Willis Street, go straight on for 100 m and then turn right at the end of the road.

A: Thanks very much.

A: Excuse me, could you tell me the way to the nearest hotel?

B: Turn around, walk straight on for 1 km and then turn left into Wall Street. Cross the street and you will see Harry's Hotel.

A: Thanks!

It is polite to begin with "Excuse me" when asking a stranger a question. "Could" is a polite way of askng "can" in questions.

9   Point to a position on the map on page 114. Imagine you are standing in this position. Tell your partner where you are and then ask for directions. Follow your partner's directions with your finger.

I am walking out of Tamara's house. Could you tell me how I get to the park, please?

10 **Follow the lines to match the words to their meaning. Circle the words in the poem below.**

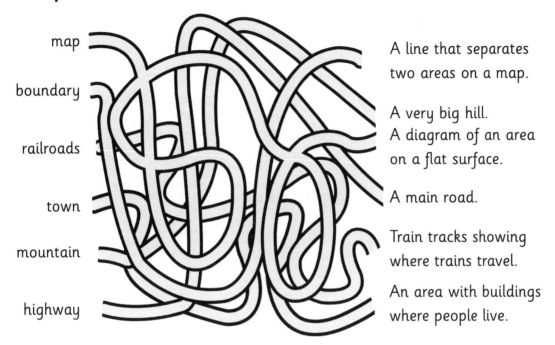

map

boundary

railroads

town

mountain

highway

A line that separates two areas on a map.

A very big hill.
A diagram of an area on a flat surface.

A main road.

Train tracks showing where trains travel.

An area with buildings where people live.

11 **Listen to the poem *Making Maps*. Fill in the missing words. Use the words in the box to help you.**

| bend | drawn | end | fun | gone | lake | make | one |

I love to make maps!

I think it's great _____,

Making the boundaries

And then one by _____

Putting in railroads.

And each river _____,

And the tiny towns

Where little roads _____.

I draw in the mountains,

And often a _____,

And I've even had

Long bridges to _____!

I like to do highways.

And when they are _____

I dream that they take me

Where I've never _____.

12 **Look at the map. Read about Mia's little town. Label the buildings and streets to match the story.**

Where is Mia's house?

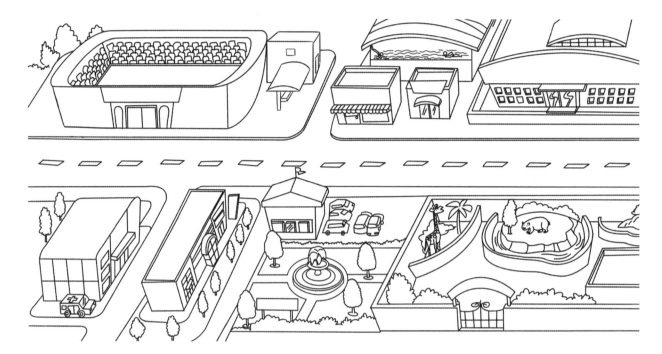

Mia lives in Tidy Town. She loves her little town. It has everything she needs.

Mia's house is next to the sports stadium and the bus stop.

The sports stadium is in Main Street.

Mia's school is next to Izzy's Ice-cream Shop in Main Street.

The ice-cream shop is next to her favourite restaurant, called Athena's.

The public swimming pool is behind Athena's restaurant.

The car park and public library are opposite Izzy's Ice-cream Shop and Athena's restaurant.

Behind the library is the park. Mia loves playing here with her friends.

To the right of the park is the zoo.

Across the road from the park is a small shopping centre.

The street between the park and the shopping centre is Clean Street.

The hospital is in Neat Street, across the street from the shopping centre.

13 **Answer these questions about Mia by crossing out the wrong answer.**

Example: Mia can swim at the public pool, can't she?

Yes, she can. ~~No, she can't.~~

a) Mia can watch football at the sport's stadium, can't she?

Yes, she can.   No, she can't.

b) Mia is sad in Tidy Town, isn't she?

Yes, she is.   No, she isn't.

c) Mia does go to the park sometimes, doesn't she?

Yes, she does.   No, she doesn't.

d) Mia loves Tidy Town, doesn't she?

Yes, she does.   No, she doesn't.

14 **Fill in the gaps to create your own questions about Mia. Then answer your questions.**

Example: Mia can _sing well_, can't she?   _No, she can't._

a) Mia can _____, can't she?   _____

b) Mia is _____, isn't she?   _____

c) Mia will _____, won't she?   _____

d) Mia likes _____, doesn't she?   _____

e) Mia doesn't like _____, does she?   _____

15 **Find and underline the prepositions in this paragraph. List the prepositions you find below.**

Sunesh loves drawing maps – he's crazy about it. He's better at it than all his friends. What are you interested in doing? Do you have hobbies that are similar to or different from your friends? Are you good or bad at the things they are keen on, or do you get bored by the things they like doing?

_____   _____   _____   _____

_____   _____   _____   _____

16 **Complete the sentences using the correct prepositions from the box. You will need to use one preposition more than once.**

about	at	by	in	of	on

a) Julie is crazy _____ her phone.

b) Are you interested _____ comics? Which ones are you most keen _____?

c) Pedro is very bad _____ maths, but he's much better _____ science.

d) I get really bored _____ my brother's friends. All they do is play games on their phones!

e) Janice is very proud _____ her football trophy.

f) Who is the best _____ drawing maps in your class?

17 **Write 'it' or 'there' to complete these sentences.**

a) _____ is great fun to go on a treasure hunt.

b) _____ are a lot of places you can go to.

c) _____ is true that you might not find treasure when you go metal detecting.

d) You may not enjoy being outside when _____ rains. I prefer to go metal detecting when _____ is sunny.

e) _____ is still a lot of hidden treasure and _____ is a lot of interest in metal detecting.

18 **Fill in the gaps to create questions to ask your partner. Then write their answers.**

Example: You can _play football, can't you?_   _Yes, I can_.

a) You can _____, _____? _____

b) You are _____, _____? _____

c) You will _____, _____? _____

d) You like _____, _____? _____

e) You don't like _____, _____? _____

Week 3 Where is it?

1 **Listen to *Mojo and Weeza and the New Hat*. Write the correct answer to complete the sentences.**

a) Mojo and Weeza looked smart _____ (in / under) their new clothes.

b) Weeza put his new hat _____ (up / on), but the wind blew it _____ (off / down).

c) The wind blew Weeza's hat far _____ (away / under).

d) Weeza looked _____ (between / off) the rocks, but it wasn't there.

e) Weeza looked _____ (out / up) the tree, but it wasn't there.

f) Weeza looked _____ (over / down) the hole, but it wasn't there either.

g) Weeza sat _____ (down / in).

h) Mojo and Weeza walked _____ (on / through) the mud to fetch the hat.

2 **What did Mojo and Weeza find? Fill in the missing word. Draw a picture to match each sentence.**

By the rocks, they found a _____.	Up the tree, they found a _____.	Down the hole, they found a _____.

3 Look at the picture of a mouse on some stairs. Draw another picture to show the mouse in a different place. Write a sentence to describe where it is.

_____

_____

_____

4 Write two negative sentences about each of these pictures. Use the words in brackets to help you.

(boy, sofa)	(rabbit, table)	(mouse, tea cup)	(cat, bed)
The boy isn't in front of the sofa.			
The boy isn't under the sofa.			

5 **Look at the picture of Megan's messy room. Read the questions and think about the answers.**

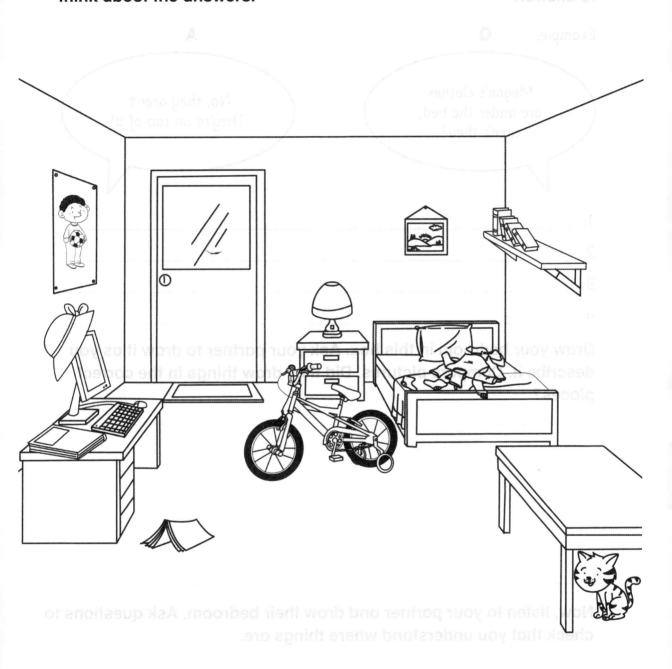

Where is the bed?	Where is the mat?
Where is the cat?	Where is the computer?
Where is the poster?	Where is the hat?
Where is the bicycle?	Where are the clothes?

6 Write questions about the picture on page 123 for your partner to answer.

Example: **Q**   **A**

Megan's clothes are under the bed, aren't they?

No, they aren't. They're on top of it!

1: _____

2: _____

3: _____

4: _____

7 Draw your bedroom in this box. Ask your partner to draw it as you describe it. Compare pictures. Did they draw things in the correct places?

Now, listen to your partner and draw their bedroom. Ask questions to check that you understand where things are.

8   **Look at this map. Where did these explorers go?**

Follow the square **down** from the letter and **across** from the number.

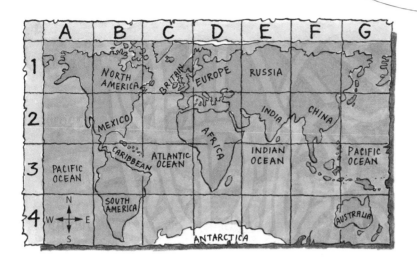

a)   The Polynesians went to _____. (G3)

b)   The Vikings went to _____ and _____. (B1 and C1)

c)   Marco Polo went to _____. (F2)

d)   Muhammad Ibn Batuta went to _____. (F2)

e)   Christopher Columbus went to _____. (B3)

f)   Ferdinand Magellan went to _____. (B4)

g)   Francis Drake went to _____. (A3)

h)   Hernan Cortez went to _____. (B2)

i)   James Cook went to _____. (G4)

j)   Samuel and Florence Baker went to _____. (D2)

k)   Roald Amundsen and Robert Scott went to _____. (D4)

9   **The adjectives in some of these sentences are in the wrong order. Correct the mistakes and tick the sentences that are right.**

a)   The early explorers had wooden, small boats. ☐

_____

b)   They made long, hard journeys across the sea. ☐

_____

c) The early explorers found the most beautiful, small islands. ☐

_____

d) They landed on sandy, white, soft beaches. ☐

_____

e) People enjoy looking at old, interesting maps. ☐

_____

f) Sometimes the maps have pictures of strange, large animals. ☐

_____

10 **Fill the gaps in the sentences with the correct form of the adverbs in brackets. You will need to change some of the adverbs.**

a) The early South-east Asian sailors sailed much _____ (far) than anyone before them.

b) She sings quite _____ (badly), though she doesn't sing the

_____ (badly) in her family!

c) I did rather _____ (well) in the quiz, but Omar did even

_____ (well) than me.

d) Heba can run as _____ (fast) as Zain, but Yasser can run much

_____ (fast) than both of them.

e) We talked too _____ (noisily) in the library and some people asked

us to talk more _____ (quietly).

f) My little brother shouted the _____ (loudly) at the match.

11 **Read the words below aloud. Cross out the word that doesn't rhyme. Make a short two-line rhyme with the words that do rhyme.**

Example: fat ~~pan~~ cat _I have a cute cat. He is very fat._

a) man van sat _____

b) wag big wig _____

c) dad mum hum _____

d) red bad bed _____

12 **Listen to this poem. Circle the words that have the same sounds. Look at how the words are spelled.**

> **Going for a Drive**
>
> We are going for a drive.
> We are glad to be alive.
>
> Right then, people, off we go.
> Vroom, vroom, vroom and cheerio.
>
> Fields and hedges, hills and trees.
> Feel the sunshine. Feel the breeze.
>
> Vroom, vroom, vroom, we're on our way.
> Vroom, vroom, vroom. Hip, hip hooray.
>
> We are going on a drive.
> We are glad to be alive.
>
> *By Wendy Cope*

> Words that sound the same are not always spelled in the same way. For example, *slow* sounds like *go* but the 'o' sound is spelled 'ow'.

13 **Write the words from the poem that have the same sounds. Then write more words that sound the same.**

a) drive _____ _____ _____

_____

b) go _____ _____ _____

_____

c) trees _____ _____ _____

_____

d) way _____ _____ _____

_____

Unit 8 Take a break

Week 1 Take a break

1 **Read *Carlos takes siestas* on page 50 of the Student's Resource Book. What do you think Carlos does every day? Complete his schedule.**

06:00 *Carlos wakes up at 06:00.* _____

06:20 _____

06:40 _____

07:30 _____

08:00 _____

08:30 _____

14:00 _____

14:30 _____

16:00 _____

19:30 _____

20:00 _____

2 **Read *Takumi needs time* on page 51 of the Student's Resource Book. Then answer these questions about Takumi and his work routine.**

a) What does Takumi do for 55 minutes in the morning?

_____

b) What does he do at lunch time?

_____

c) What does he do to help him concentrate?

_____

d) When does he go home?

_____

e) What does he do when he gets home?

_____

f) When does he exercise?

_____

g) Why do you think the story is called *Takumi needs time?*

_____

3 **What are some of the activities that you do every day?**

   a) In the morning, I _____

   b) I also _____

   c) In the afternoon, _____

   d) After lunch, _____

   e) Before dinner, _____

   f) _____

   g) _____

4 **Circle the correct words to complete the paragraph.**

Carlos goes home for lunch, (so / but) Takumi has his lunch at the office. After lunch, Carlos has a short break (but / because) the shop is closed until 4pm. Sometimes Takumi feels tired in the afternoon (as / so) he has a cup of coffee. He cooks his dinner (when / then) he gets home in the evening.

5 **Use the words in the box to complete the paragraph about Dina's day. You can use the words more than once.**

> after   and   at   before   in   on   so   when

Dina lives in Cairo. _____ school days, she gets up _____ 6am. _____ she has a shower, she gets dressed and has breakfast. She leaves home _____ 7am _____ she can be at school _____ it starts.

She has a break at 11.30 am, _____ she has lunch. She usually buys a sandwich _____ eats it in the school canteen. She sometimes buys some snacks _____ break time _____ she has something to eat _____ she gets home. School finishes _____ 2pm. Dina does her homework _____ home _____ the afternoon. _____ the end of the day, she watches TV.

6 **Write a paragraph in your notebook to describe your daily routine.**

7 These words were made by joining two words together. Write the two words that were joined together.

A compound noun is a noun that is made up of two or more words. For example, 'handbag'.

a) sunshine = _____ + _____

b) toothpaste = _____ + _____

c) seafood = _____ + _____

d) football = _____ + _____

e) fireflies = _____ + _____

f) summertime = _____ + _____

8 Join these words together to make new words.

a) white + board = _____

b) bath + room = _____

c) down + stairs = _____

d) break + fast = _____

e) sun + rise = _____

f) hair + cut = _____

9 Write sentences for three of the words above.

a) _____

b) _____

c) _____

10 Discuss these questions with your partner:

Why do you think some people like going to the beach for the summer holiday?

What are some fun things you can do at the beach?

11 **Listen to *Horses' Holiday*. Write 'true' or 'false'.**

    a) *Horses' Holiday* is a poem. _____

    b) It is about different types of animals that go on holiday. _____

    c) The horses need transport to their holiday. _____

    d) Only children are allowed on the horses' holiday. _____

    e) The horses are sad at the beginning. _____

    f) The horses are sorry at the end. _____

12 **Luke is telling his friend Imran about his family's holiday. Circle the present simple forms and underline the present continuous forms.**

> We can use present tenses to talk about things in the future for planned and scheduled events. Examples:
>
> We **are visiting** our cousins in the summer. (planned event – present continuous)
>
> The concert **starts** at 7 o'clock. (scheduled event – present simple)

We're going on holiday next week. We're going to the beach. We leave on Tuesday and we are catching the train. Our train leaves at 9 o'clock in the morning and we arrive at 12 o'clock. We're staying in a hotel opposite the beach. We are staying there for five days and come back next Sunday.

13 **Choose the correct form of the verbs to complete these sentences.**

    a) The bus (leaves / is leaving) on Friday at 10am.

    b) My dad (goes / is going) to Morocco with my uncle in the summer.

    c) We (are taking / take) a train to Istanbul.

    d) The film (starts / is starting) at 8pm tomorrow.

    e) The beach volleyball match (begins / is beginning) today after lunch.

    f) My brother (enters / is entering) the dance competition this evening.

14 **Listen to *Summer holidays*. Underline the things you hear about.**

beach ball   birds   butterflies   fireflies   park   picnic   rain   river   sea
seashells   sun cream   watermelon   wind

15 **Unscramble these words from *Summer holidays*. Write the words and match them to the correct picture.**

| d | neuishsn | sunshine |

| | ebach labl | _____ |

| | easlhslse | _____ |

| | tilghhsoue | _____ |

| | sila btoa | _____ |

| | snu crmae | _____ |

| | cheba gab | _____ |

| | eamnwrlteo | _____ |

| | btooflla | _____ |

| | ttuberlefis | _____ |

| | freiilefs | _____ |

a)

b)

d)

c)

f)

e)

h)

g)

j)

i)

k)

16 Choose five of the pictures on pages 52–53 of the Student's Resource Book and describe what the horses are doing. You can use words from the poem to help you.

1: _____

2: _____

3: _____

4: _____

5: _____

Describe the pictures to your partner. Can they identify them?

17 Read these sentences. Answer the questions.

a) Summer is too hot. Summer days are long and lazy.

Do you think the writer likes summer? Why?

_____

b) Summer is warm and sunny. Summer days are long and full of fun.

Do you think the writer likes summer? Why?

_____

18 What do you think of summer? Write a paragraph or a poem.

_____

_____

_____

_____

_____

_____

_____

_____

Week 2 Exciting destinations

1 Complete the sentences with the best ending.

We wanted to eat pizza •

The basketball team won •

I can dance, •

You may play outside •

We always have a good time •

• when you have finished your homework.

• when we visit our cousins.

• because they practised hard.

• so we went to our local restaurant.

• but I can't sing.

> Connectives are joining words. They join words or sentences.

2 Read *Travel to Spain for La Tomatina* on page 54 in the Student's Resource Book. List the different connectives you can find.

_____   _____   _____   _____

_____   _____

3 Read *Travel to Kenya to see wild animals* on page 54 in the Student's Resource Book. List the different connectives you can find.

_____   _____   _____   _____

_____   _____

4 Read these connectives. Make up a sentence with each one.

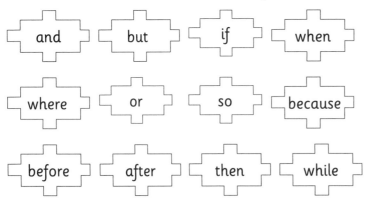

and   but   if   when

where   or   so   because

before   after   then   while

> Think about how you use these connectives.

5 Read *Travel to Mongolia for a camel trek* on page 55 in the Student's Resource Book. Answer the questions in full sentences.

    a) What is a nomad?

    _____

    b) Would you like to be a nomad? Why?

    _____

    c) Would you like to camel trek in Mongolia? Why?

    _____

6 Write five words that describe a camel trekking holiday.

    _____   _____   _____

    _____   _____

7 Read *Holiday at home* on page 55 in the Student's Resource Book. Answer the questions in full sentences.

    a) What can you do if you stay at home for the holiday?

    _____

    b) What are your three favourite things to do at home?

    _____   _____   _____

    c) What is a couch potato?

    _____

    d) Do you think being a couch potato is a good or bad thing? Why?

    _____

    e) Is this the perfect holiday for you? Why?

    _____

8 Write five words that describe a stay-at-home holiday.

    _____   _____   _____

    _____   _____

9 **Complete these sentences using connectives. Read the sentences to your partner.**

Use each connective only once.

Example: I usually eat pasta _or_ rice with my dinner.

a) Baby lions are cute, _____ they are dangerous.

b) Gabriel cried _____ he was very sad.

c) _____ school every day, I play sport _____ do my homework.

d) _____ school every day, I pack my lunch _____ I will not be hungry.

e) _____ I am older, I want to be a doctor.

f) _____ you play in the rain, you may get sick.

g) I want to live in a house _____ I can see the sea from my window.

10 **Join these short sentences to make one long sentence. Use the words in the box to help you.**

| and | because | so |

The boy ran fast. <u>The boy</u> fell over.

The boy ran fast **so** <u>he</u> fell over.

The boy fell over **because** <u>he</u> ran fast.

Sometimes more than one answer is possible.

a) Lyla likes lions. Lyla likes elephants.

_____

b) Aba and Gabriel are hungry. Aba and Gabriel didn't eat lunch.

_____

c) I feel tired. I feel sick. I feel hungry.

_____

d) You need to eat vegetables. You need to exercise every day. You can be healthy.

_____

11 **Look at the texts on pages 54–55 in the Student's Resource Book again and read these sentences. Circle the correct option.**

1   *La Tomatina* is an Italian festival.

    a) Right   **b)** Wrong   **c)** Doesn't say

2   You can see many wild animals in Kenya.

    a) Right   **b)** Wrong   **c)** Doesn't say

3   A camel trek in Mongolia lasts for one month.

    a) Right   **b)** Wrong   **c)** Doesn't say

4   'Couch potato' is a name for a person who eats a lot of potatoes.

    a) Right   **b)** Wrong   **c)** Doesn't say

5   *La Tomatina* happens every year, in April.

    a) Right   **b)** Wrong   **c)** Doesn't say

6   A nomad moves around a lot and lives in many different places.

    a) Right   **b)** Wrong   **c)** Doesn't say

12 **Read pages 54–55 of the Student's Resource Book again. Join the beginning of a sentence with the correct ending to describe each holiday.**

a) If you don't mind getting dirty   •   • if you're not feeling adventurous.

b) If you prefer watching wild animals •   • go to Spain for *La Tomatina*!

c) Head for the Mongolian desert   •   • a safari holiday is for you!

d) You can stay at home   •   • if you want to sleep under the stars.

13 **Write two sentences of your own describing two of the holidays using 'if'.**

If _____

_____

_____ if _____

_____

14 Follow these instructions.

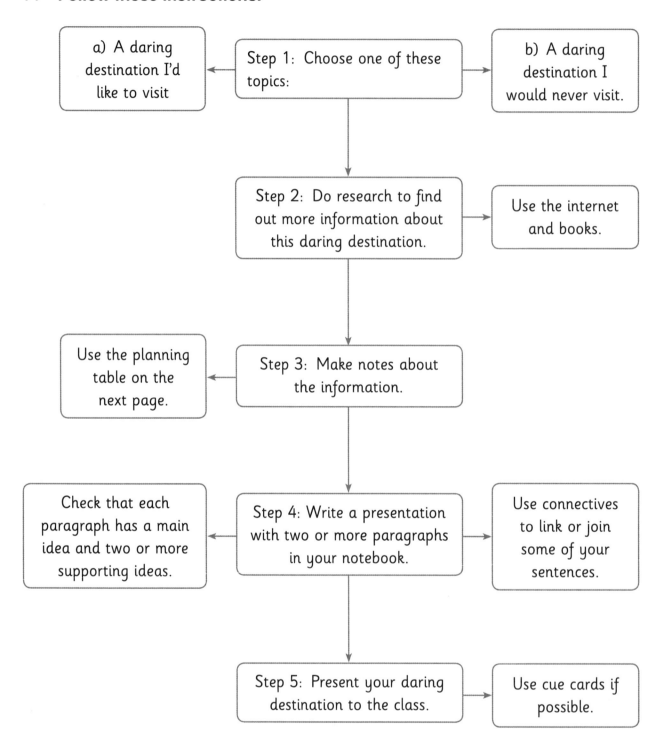

a) A daring destination I'd like to visit

Step 1: Choose one of these topics:

b) A daring destination I would never visit.

Step 2: Do research to find out more information about this daring destination.

Use the internet and books.

Use the planning table on the next page.

Step 3: Make notes about the information.

Check that each paragraph has a main idea and two or more supporting ideas.

Step 4: Write a presentation with two or more paragraphs in your notebook.

Use connectives to link or join some of your sentences.

Step 5: Present your daring destination to the class.

Use cue cards if possible.

MY PLANNING

Name of daring destination:

Picture:

Location:

Characteristics:

Daring because:

Activities:

Fun facts:

Why I would / wouldn't like to visit it:

Week 3 Let's travel together

1   **Read the holiday stories on pages 56–57 in the Student's Resource Book. Write words that describe these holidays.**

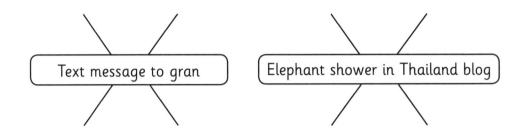

2   **Imagine you are writing a blog about one of the holidays in the Student's Resource Book. Describe what you are doing today.**

Blog title: _____   Date: _____

Today I am in _____ (place) and I am excited to see _____

First, I am _____

Then, _____

After lunch, _____

And after that, _____

3   **Imagine you can go on holiday tomorrow.**

What type of holiday will you choose? _____

Where will you go? _____

How long will you go for? _____

Who will you go with? _____

List three things you will do on holiday:

I will _____.

I will _____.

I will _____.

4   **Draw a picture of an adventure you had on your last holiday.**

5   **Write a blog post about an adventure you had on your last holiday.**

Title:

By: Date:

_____

_____

_____

_____

_____

_____

_____

_____

_____

_____

6 **Plan a perfect holiday in groups.**

We are going to _____ because _____.	Type of holiday: _____
We are going for _____ days.	While we are there, we will _____ and we will _____, but we won't _____.
We are going to pack: _____ _____ _____ _____ _____ _____	While we are there, we won't _____ or _____, but we will _____.
We will eat _____.	We will see _____.
We are travelling by _____.	

7 **Present your perfect holiday to the class.**

8 **Imagine that you are on your perfect holiday. You decide to write a letter to your best friend, to tell him or her all about your amazing holiday.**

- How have you been travelling from one place to another?

- What have you been doing? What have you seen?

- What have been the best and worst parts of the holiday?

- What are you going to do next? What are you excited about doing or trying?

9 **Read this paragraph about Bill and Grace. Complete each sentence with 'for' or 'since'.**

Bill and Grace have been married _____ 50 years. They have travelled every holiday _____ the day they got married. Grace has written in her travel journal _____ they started travelling. Bill has packed the suitcases _____ the last ten years. _____ they began to travel, Grace has always planned the holidays. They have visited more than 30 countries!

Bill and Grace have lived in three countries. They lived in Scotland _____ most of their lives. They lived in Malaysia _____ four years and now they live in Nigeria. They have lived here _____ March, 2014. Grace has been a teacher _____ she was 24 years old. She loves children. She has taught in many different schools _____ she met Bill. Bill has been a doctor _____ 52 years. He loves helping sick people. He has helped people all around the world _____ a very long time. _____ he started working, Bill has always relaxed on Sundays.

10 **Use the words in the box to help you complete these sentences.**

> that   when   where   who   whose

a) Nigeria is _____ they live now.

b) Bill is the person _____ packs the suitcases.

c) Teaching is the job _____ Grace does.

d) Grace is the woman _____ job is a teacher.

e) Her travel journal is the book _____ Grace writes in.

f) The holidays are the time _____ Bill and Grace travel.

g) Scotland is _____ they both grew up.

h) Bill's Sundays are _____ he relaxes.

Unit 9 Breaking records

Champions

1   **Read the introduction to *Rising above the challenge* on page 58 in the Student's Resource Book. Discuss these questions.**

What do you know about the Olympic Games?

Have you ever watched the Olympic Games?

Which events do you enjoy the most? Why?

Which events do you enjoy the least? Why?

2   **Fill in the missing gaps with 'There' or 'It'.**

The Olympic Games is an event that happens every four years.

a) _____ are a lot of talented competitors.

b) _____ is difficult to make an Olympic team.

c) _____ is a lot of hard work to do before you are good enough to enter.

d) _____ are many countries represented at the Games.

e) When one Games ends, _____ is time to start training for the next one.

f) _____ can cost a lot of money to train properly.

3   **Label the pictures.**

archery   boxing   diving   gymnastics   rowing

a)   **b)**   **c)**   **d)**   **e)**

_____   _____   _____   _____   _____

145

4 **Complete the table to rate the sports in Activity 3.**

Watching the sport		Doing the sport	
1 (like the most)	_____	1 (like the most)	_____
2	_____	2	_____
3	_____	3	_____
4	_____	4	_____
5 (like the least)	_____	5 (like the least)	_____

5 **Complete these sentences.**

a) I don't really enjoy watching _____ because _____.

b) I love watching _____ the most because _____.

c) I would not want to do _____ because _____.

d) I would really love to do _____ because _____.

6 **This glossary from a book about Olympic heroes is muddled. Draw a line to match the word to the correct meaning.**

Reading the words in context may help you to work out the meaning. A dictionary will also help you.

bobsleigh   Unfair feelings or opinions.

champions   To take part in a competition.

compete   An injury or something you are born with, which can make it difficult for you to move freely.

disability   People who have won in a competition.

operation   A sledge used for racing over snow or ice.

Paralympics   Medical treatment by a surgeon.

prejudice   The bones in your back.

spine   Olympic Games for differently-abled athletes.

7 Read *Brave Beginners* and *Winning Wheels* on page 59 of the Student's Resource Book, and complete the table about these Olympic and Paralympic heroes and the challenges they overcame.

	Name	Challenges	Achievements

8 Answer these questions in full sentences.

a) Where were the first modern Olympics held?

b) Who won the first medal?

c) In which sport did the Jamaican team compete in 1988?

d) Why was it difficult for the Jamaican team to compete?

e) Who entered her first wheelchair race when she was 13?

f) Why did this champion have to stop training?

g) What are the Paralympic Games?

_____

h) Why are the people in this article called 'heroes'?

_____

9 **Write questions that match these answers.**

Example: _When were the first Olympics held?_

The first Olympics were held in 1896.

a) _____

The first Winter Olympics were held in 1924.

b) _____

They were from Jamaica.

c) _____

She had an orange wheelchair.

d) _____

Tanni Grey-Thompson won 16 medals in the Paralympic Games.

10 **Read the paragraph below with your partner and underline the quantifiers.**

Most people love playing sport. Many people enjoy competing in sport competitions, like running, swimming and cycling. Not as many people work really, really hard to become champions in the sport they love. Even fewer people will spend their whole lives training to become the best. It is very difficult to be the best in your country, and even more difficult to be the best in the world. Very few people win medals in the Olympics. Those people who do win medals are remarkable champions.

A quantifier is a word that tells us how much there is of something. For example, _some, most, few, not enough, even more._

11 **Circle the correct answer.**

1 More people   **a)** love playing sport than competing in competitions.

b) enjoy competing in competitions than love playing sport.

2 More people   **a)** win medals in the Olympics than watch the Olympics on television.

b) watch the Olympics on television than win medals in the Olympics.

3 Not as many people   **a)** live in France as in the rest of the world.

b) live in the rest of the world as in France.

12 **Underline the best words to complete these sentences.**

a) (Many / Not as many) people like to play sports sometimes, but (many / not as many) people play sports every day.

b) (Few / Fewer) people play a sport for eight hours every day, and (few / fewer) people become Olympic champions.

c) I don't watch a lot of sport, I only watch a (little / less).

d) I love soccer! I like hockey too, but (less / not as much) as soccer.

e) Towns have (more / most) schools than sports stadiums.

f) Harold trains for three hours every day. Gerry trains for one hour every day. Gerry trains (more / less) than Harold.

13 **Listen to these ideas for a classroom Olympics. Try them out and see who gets the highest score.**

Bin-ball	Fly-far
Step 1: Crumple three pieces of paper into balls.	Step 1: Create your own paper aeroplane.
Step 2: Put your class bin in an open area.	Step 2: Draw a line at the front of the classroom.
Step 3: Draw a distance marker line 2 m from the bin.	Step 3: Five learners stand behind the line.
Step 4: Stand behind the line. Try to throw your paper ball in the bin.	Step 4: Throw your paper planes as far as possible.

Bin-ball Scoring:	Fly-far Scoring:
2 points: in the bin	3 points: for the farthest plane
1 point: hit the bin, but landed outside	2 points: for the second farthest plane
0 points: out of the bin	1 point: for the third farthest plane.
	0 points: for the planes that came fourth and fifth

14 **Create two new games and explain them to your partner. Remember to give your game a name and to explain how the scoring works.**

_____	_____
Step 1: _____	Step 1: _____
Step 2: _____	Step 2: _____
Step 3: _____	Step 3: _____
Step 4: _____	Step 4: _____
Scoring:	**Scoring:**
points: _____ _____	points: _____ _____
points: _____ _____	points: _____ _____
points: _____ _____	points: _____ _____

15 **Look at this contents page. Discuss the questions with your partner.**

What is the title of the book?

Who wrote the book?

What do you think the book is about?

Do you think the photograph was taken at the Summer or Winter Olympics? Why?

On which page can you read about Olympic heroes who have been ill?

What can you read about on page 14?

What else can you read about?

On which page is the glossary?

What is a glossary?

Olympic Heroes

Contents

Written by Jillian Powell

Collins

Week 2 Try, try and try again

1 Listen to the information about Sonja Henie. Which sentence best describes the writer's opinion of Sonja Henie?

a) ☐ Sonja was lazy and untalented.

b) ☐ Sonja needed to practise less often.

c) ☐ Sonja worked hard to become a famous skater.

2 Read about Sonja Henie. Then, write three sentences about her in your notebook. Use your own words.

> Sonja Henie was born in 1912 in Norway. The first time Sonja competed in the Olympics was when she was just 11. She is famous for being the youngest Olympic skater.
>
> Sonja won an Olympic gold medal in three Olympic Games. She was world champion ten times and she was the European champion six times. She also became a famous film star.
>
> Sonja was a very talented skater. Skating came naturally to her but she also worked very hard to become so good. She practised ice-skating for many hours every day. She often tripped. She often fell hard on the ice. She often hurt herself. But every time Sonja fell, she got up and tried again until she got it right.

3 Circle the correct adjective and fill in the missing words to complete these sentences.

a) The (amazed / amazing) Sonja Henie was a famous _____ and _____.

b) This (captivated / captivating) skater won _____ Olympic gold medals, she won the world championship _____ times and the European championship _____ times.

c) Skating came _____ to the (talent / talented) Sonja.

d) While practising, this (dedicating / dedicated) skater often _____, fell hard on the ice and _____ herself.

e) But this (hard-working / hard-workerd) skater never gave up. She always _____ again until she got it right!

4 **Match these pictures to the sentences.**

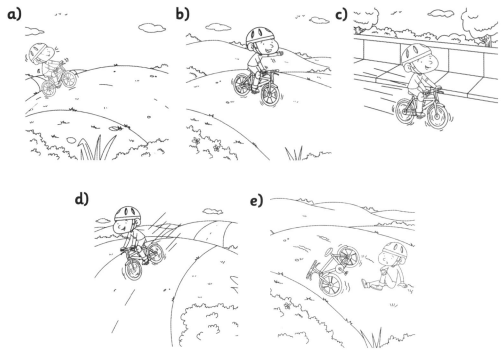

a)
b)
c)
d)
e)

1 ☐ Kamil is really passionate about cycling. He loves riding his bike.

2 ☐ When he rides downhill, he can go so fast! This is fun, but sometimes a little scary.

3 ☐ Sometimes he must ride uphill. This can be very difficult and tiring.

4 ☐ Sometimes he falls off his bicycle. This can hurt a lot.

5 ☐ Usually, Kamil likes to ride on flat roads, as fast as he can.

5 **What do you think?**

1 Circle the answer that you think is correct.

When Kamil falls off his bike,

a) he kicks his bike and puts it away for a month.

b) he gets back on again and tries to ride home.

c) he walks home and never rides again.

2 Why do you think this?

_____

3 What do you do if you fall off a bike?

_____

6 **Complete these sentences to write about an activity you are passionate about.**

a) I'm passionate about _____.

b) Sometimes it is easy to do, like when _____.

c) Sometimes it is difficult to do, like when _____.

d) I enjoy _____.

7 **Read this article and answer the question.**

Usually when we want to get better at something we have to work really hard at it. Sometimes we make mistakes, but we must never give up!

Can you remember learning how to walk? Probably not! But I am sure you fell over many times before you could walk well.

Can you remember learning how to ride a bicycle? Or how to read and write? Do you think you could do those things right the first time? Of course not! We all make many mistakes before we can do something well.

Which sentence best describes the writer's opinion?

a) ☐ We must not make mistakes because they are wrong.

b) ☐ It is normal to make mistakes when we are learning something new.

c) ☐ If you make a mistake, you need to stop trying to learn that thing.

8 **Write down three difficult things you have learned to do. Then, write about why each one was difficult to do.**

Example: _Learning to walk_   _I fell over many times._

Learning to use chopsticks   _My food went everywhere!_

a) _____   _____

b) _____   _____

c) _____   _____

9 **Listen to *First Day*.**

a) Write the character's name next to the picture.

b) Match the characters to their job and write it under their name.

c) Describe what the character did wrong. Begin with *He* or *She*.

1 Name: _____

Job: _____

She _____.

2 Name: _____

Job: _____

He _____.

3 Name: _____

Job: _____

_____.

4 Name: _____

Job: _____

_____.

5 Name: _____

Job: _____

hairdresser

builder

farm worker

zookeeper

gardener

_____.

10 **Follow these instructions to help you plan and write a funny story about someone who starts a new job.**

Step 1: Describe the main character.

Name: _____

Be creative.

Age: _____

New job: _____

Words to describe this character: _____ _____

_____

Step 2: Plan the content.

Write three things your character *needs to* do on the first day of the new job.

_____

_____

_____

Write three things that went horribly wrong on the first day.

_____

_____

_____

Step 3: Plan the ending.

Does your story have a happy or sad ending? _____

What happens in the end?

_____

Step 4: Write your story in your note book.

Use paragraphs.

Remember

Check spelling.

Punctuate carefully.

Step 5: Write three questions about your story in your notebook.

Step 6: Read your story to your group. Then ask your questions.

Did your classmates listen well? How do you know?

Week 3 Ridiculous records

1 **Read these sentences. Circle the words 'at', 'in' and 'on'.**

a) The Guinness World Records started in 1955.

b) My birthday is on 5 March, 2011.

c) On Saturdays, we go to the park and play football.

d) School finishes at 4 o'clock every day.

e) They broke the record in 14 minutes.

f) At lunch time, the teachers meet and eat lunch together.

g) In the afternoon, the teachers meet and talk about their students.

h) It sometimes snows in winter.

i) My little brother started school in September.

2 **We use 'at', 'in' and 'on' in front of time phrases. Use Activity 1 to help you sort these phrases into the correct clock.**

o'clock   dates   days   length of time   months   mealtimes

part of the day   season   time   years

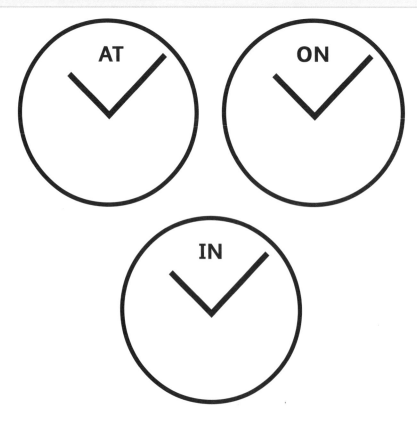

3 **Complete these sentences with 'at', 'in' or 'on'.**

a) My dad wakes me up _____ 7 o'clock every morning.

b) I often feel tired _____ the afternoon.

c) Sarah will visit her grandmother _____ Wednesday.

d) Zack is going to Brazil _____ the 17th of July.

e) My birthday is _____ March.

f) _____ 1896, the first modern Olympic Games was held in Athens.

g) We always go skiing _____ winter.

4 **Listen to *How to get into the Guinness World Records book*. Discuss these questions.**

How many records has Ashrita Furman set?

What is the first thing you need to do if you want to set a new record?

What is the last thing you must do?

How many steps are there in total?

5 **Use words from the box to fill the gaps to show the correct order of the sentences.**

| And finally | Fifth | First | Fourth | Second | Sixth | Third |

a) _____, check with the people at Guinness World Records and ask them if your idea is okay.

b) _____, send your video and documents to Guinness World Records.

c) _____, when you are ready, get people to come and watch your event.

d) _____, choose a record that you want to break.

e) _____, wait for them to send you an official certificate.

f) _____, exercise and practise often.

g) _____, remember to record yourself, as proof you really did it.

6 **Read these instructions.**

How to make toast	
A	**B**
Put a slice of bread in the toaster. You can add cheese, butter, jam, honey or anything. If the toast burns then you've left the toast in for too long and you will have to throw it away and start again. If the toast doesn't brown, your toaster isn't switched on so you must plug it in and switch it on. Add the toppings and wait for the toast to pop. Enjoy.	It is easy to make toast if you follow these steps. First, make sure that your toaster is plugged in and switched on. Secondly, set the temperature dial. Next, put a slice of bread in the toaster. Then, wait until the toast pops up. After that, remove your slice of bread from the toaster and put it on a plate. Finally, add toppings to create a tasty snack.

a) Which instructions are easy to follow? Why?

_____

b) Which words help to order the steps and link one idea to the next?

_____

7 **Read the linking words in the box. Use them in sentences in Activity 8.**

8 **Choose one of these topics. Write instructions.**

How to make a cup of tea

How to send a text message on your phone

How to be a good friend

It is easy to _____ if you follow these steps.

> (To begin)
> First, / Firstly, /
> To begin with, / First of all,
>
> (To continue)
> Second, / Secondly, / Then, /
> Next, / After this, / And then,
>
> (To end)
> Lastly, / Finally, / To finish,

a) _____ , _____

b) _____ , _____

c) _____ , _____

d) _____ , _____

e) _____ , _____

f) _____ , _____

9   **What do you love to do? Write simple instructions about how to do it.**

Follow these _____ steps to help you learn how to _____.

_____

_____

_____

_____

_____

_____

_____

_____

10 **Read these opinions.**

a) Which opinions do you agree with? Why?

_____

b) Which opinions do you disagree with? Why?

_____

I believe that all learners need to have a smartphone. One reason is, it saves us time.

I think South Africa is an interesting place to visit. This is because there are many exciting things to see. One example is, you can go on a game drive to see wild animals.

In my opinion, summer is better than winter. One reason is, I like to play summer sports. For example, I really enjoy playing cricket.

11 **Now write your own opinion about two of these topics. Use the words in the box to help you.**

watching television _____

learning English _____

playing sport _____

doing homework _____

> I think that ... / In my opinion,
>
> This is because ... / One reason is,
>
> For example, / ..., such as ...

12 **Discuss your topic and opinion with your partner. Do they agree or disagree with you?**

13 **Research Guinness World Records. Find a record that interests you. Write a plan about how you would break this record. Use linking words and try to write at least five steps.**

My plan is to break _____.

The current record is _____.

_____

_____

_____

_____

_____

_____